# Effective HR Measurement Techniques

# Effective HR Measurement Techniques

Edited by Maureen J. Fleming & Jennifer B. Wilson

Society for Human Resource Management
Alexandria, Virginia
USA
www.shrm.org

This book is published by the Society for Human Resource Management (SHRM®) and funded by a grant from the SHRM Foundation. The interpretations, conclusions, and recommendations in this book are those of the author and do not necessarily represent those of SHRM or the SHRM Foundation.

ISBN 1-58644-018-7

The Society for Human Resource Management (SHRM) is the leading voice of the human resource profession, representing more than 160,000 professional and student members throughout the world. Visit SHRM Online at www.shrm.org.

As the R&D arm of the profession, the SHRM Foundation expands the body of human resource knowledge through its support of leading-edge research, practical publications, and education initiatives. Visit SHRM Foundation online at www.shrm.org/foundation.

# Table of Contents

# Preface

The Society for Human Resource Management (SHRM) Research Committee fosters the use of applied research in human resources and identifies ways to facilitate the use of data. The primary goal of this book is to demystify measurement techniques so that human resource practitioners can use those techniques in the daily operation of their human resource offices and in communicating with other members in their organizations.

To those ends we have included chapters that apply common, traditional standards of measurement to real challenges facing practitioners. We have also included chapters on new developments in the human resource research and measurement fields that are closer to the cutting edge. We hope you will find answers to some of your questions in this book. We have also recommended additional readings and resources to help you in answering your more complex questions.

No successful book can be created and published without the vision, talent, and cooperation of a team, and we would like to acknowledge and thank our contributors. Our core team consisted of members of the research committee and invited authors who volunteered their time and effort to write and refine the chapters. We cannot thank them enough for their ideas and good humor throughout the project. James R. Jose, PhD, SPHR, chair of the SHRM Research Committee, supported our work from beginning to end. Special thanks go to Anne Iverson for refining and organizing the chapters in an initial edit of the book. We also want to acknowledge the SHRM staff members at the national office for their role in taking the edited document and moving it through the publication process to produce the book you have in your hands. Finally, we thank the SHRM Foundation for believing in the value of the project and for providing the funding for the printing of the book. We hope you find the efforts of the combined team to be valuable in your work.

Maureen J. Fleming, PhD　　Jennifer B. Wilson, PhD, SPHR
Editor　　　　　　　　　　　Editor

# About the Authors

## Sara Brown, PhD

Sara Brown is a senior organization development consultant with Good Work Associates in New Haven, Connecticut. She has also held positions as training and organization development manager at the *Los Angeles Times* and as vice president of human resources at The Columbian in Vancouver, Washington. Dr. Brown, an adjunct professor at the University of New Haven School of Business and a lecturer at Quinnipiac University, has presented and published articles on 360-degree feedback and other organization development and human resources (HR) issues. She also writes a monthly column on management for *Publishers Auxiliary*. Ms. Brown holds a PhD in Human and Organization Systems from the Fielding Institute, an MS in Human Resources and Organization Development from the University of San Francisco, and a BS in Management Development from Marylhurst College.

## Heidi Connole

Heidi Connole received a BA in Psychology and a BS in Marketing in 1994 from the University of Montana and an MBA in 1995. She taught at the University of Montana for several years before beginning the PhD program in International Business at Washington State University in 1998. She has taught courses in International Management, Organizational Behavior, and Business Strategy. Ms. Connole is a member of the Academy of Management and the Academy of International Business and has worked extensively in the private sector as a management and marketing consultant in a variety of industries, including nonprofit organizations. She is a U.S. Army veteran of the Persian Gulf War and is conducting research in the areas of leadership and entrepreneurship among nontraditional populations.

## Maureen J. Fleming, PhD

Maureen Fleming is a professor of management at the University of Montana. She received a bachelor of arts degree in 1963 from Mundelein College, along with a master's degree in 1966 and a doctorate in 1969 from Southern Illinois University. An active member of the Big Sky chapter of the Society for Human Resource Management (SHRM), Dr. Fleming has been involved in the organization and its predecessor, ASPA, for more than 20 years. Dr. Fleming, an international consultant, is a member of SHRM's national research committee, the Academy of Management, the Academy of International Business, the Association of Global Business, the Association of Marketing Theory and Practice, and the International Association of Business Disciplines. She also serves as a trustee for the Montana Board of Investment. Dr. Fleming has been widely published in the journals of the organizations in which she has memberships.

## Daniel G. Gallagher, PhD

Daniel G. Gallagher is the CSX Corporation professor of management at James Madison University in Harrisonburg, Virginia. Professor Gallagher earned his MA and PhD degrees at the Institute of Labor and Industrial Relations at the University of Illinois with concentrations in the areas of industrial psychology and economics. Dr. Gallagher's research career has focused on a range of topics, including impasse resolution procedures, compensation systems, justice, organizational and union commitment, part-time employment, psychological contracts, and most recently, the growth and implications of contingent and flexible employment arrangements. His work has been widely published in such journals as *Industrial and Labor Relations Review, Academy of Management Journal, Industrial Relations, Journal of Organizational Behavior, Human Resource Management Review,* and *Journal of Applied Psychology.*

## Jeffrey R. Hoffmann

Jeffrey Hoffmann has 20 years of experience in leadership, job design, selection, training, organizational development, international relations, market research, and chemical engineering. Mr. Hoffmann is the president of a British-owned firm for which he is conducting the North American start-up. Before that, he was president of a manufacturing firm at which he led a successful turnaround. Mr. Hoffmann received his BS in Psychology from Ramapo College and his MA in Industrial/Organizational Psychology from Montclair State College. He has spoken at universities and national seminars on corporate mission and leadership and on organizational culture, and he is an active member of the Society for Human Resource Management, the American Psychological Association, the Society for Industrial and Organizational Psychology, the Organizational Development Network, and the American Society for Training and Development.

## Rose Howse, SPHR, CCP

Rose Howse received her associate's degree in 1988 from Oakland Community College in Farmington Hills, as well as a BS degree in 1991 and an MLIR degree in 1994 from Michigan State University. Ms. Howse worked with Herman Miller, Inc., as a senior compensation specialist and with Cascade Engineering, Inc., where she served in HR management, HRIS, apprenticeship project leadership, compensation management, and HR research roles. She authored and co-authored Cascade's successful bids in 1999 for the Ron Brown Award for Corporate Leadership (administered by The Conference Board and sponsored by the U.S. Department of Commerce) and in 1998 for Michigan Manufacturer of the Year (awarded by the Michigan Manufacturers' Association). Under the mentorship of her sociology professor, Ms. House served as critical thinking specialist for Oakland Community College, working with students and professors on incorporating critical thinking in curriculum and writing assignments. Before pursuing advanced education and her HR career, Ms. Howse worked as a press operator and forklift driver at Washer's Incorporated, now known as Alpha Stamping, a supplier to the automotive industry. Ms. Howse concentrates her HR interests in metrics, systems development, work design, and employee relations. She is a member of SHRM's national research committee and the American Compensation Association.

## James R. Jose, PhD, SPHR

James Jose is an organizational strategist and leadership coach who heads a nationwide private practice in organizational effectiveness and strategic leadership development. He and his associates provide services to diverse organizations in the areas of organizational assessment and strategic intervention, executive coaching, leadership, team and individual development, and culture change and transition management. Dr. Jose received his BA in 1960 from Mount Union College and a master's degree and a PhD in 1962 and 1968, respectively, from The American University. He earned the coveted Senior Professional in Human Resources (SPHR) lifetime certification from the Society for Human Resource Management. Before entering private practice, Dr. Jose served in executive and leadership positions in the HR area in private industry, higher education, and government. He is an active member of SHRM at the local, regional, and national levels and serves on the senior advisory board of the Anchorage SHRM, on the board of directors of the Northwest Human Resources Management Association as the professional development director, and as chair of the SHRM national research committee and member of the board of directors of the SHRM Foundation.

## Sharafat (Shaz) Khan, PhD

Shaz Khan is a principal of the Strategy Group at Deloitte & Touche. As a consultant, he has strategized, conceptualized, and implemented HR shared services delivery models, including call center applications and supporting processes and technology. He also has made presentations on emerging business practices, shared services, HR strategies, call centers, HR technologies, and emerging HR and corporate center roles. Dr. Khan has conducted research and studies on issues surrounding strategic and tactical goals, including the creation of work design that supports business innovation and quality through empowerment. His publications, which address a variety of HR topics, include *Advanced Leader Training, Problem Handling Strategy for High Technology Office Environments*, and *The People Process: A Guide to Human Resources Management*. In addition to being an invited speaker and presenter at the federal government's National Performance Review, Dr. Khan has participated in the G-7 conference and the Future of the American Workplace conference convened by the President of the United States, working with many governmental agencies to implement improvements to customer and quality service standards within those agencies. He has received numerous awards, including the Human Resources Strategies Group's HR Compass Award from Deloitte & Touche for leadership and innovation. He is a member of the American Management Association, Association for Quality and Participation, Society for Human Resources Management, American Society of Training and Development, and National Association for Wholesaler-Distributors. Dr. Khan received his PhD from Western Michigan University in Educational Leadership. He also attended the Harvard University Graduate School of Business Administration, where he pursued Advanced Management Studies.

## Eric Anton Kreuter, MA, CPA, CMA, CFE, SPHR

Eric Anton Kreuter is a director and shareholder at Marden, Harrison & Kreuter, CPAs, PC. He received a BS in 1981 from Manhattan College and an MA in 1990 from Long Island University. Mr. Kreuter's primary HR expertise is in the areas of recruitment, compensation, performance appraisal, and counseling. His research focuses on cost control, workplace efficiency, and career planning. In addition to his primary work responsibilities, Mr. Kreuter is employed as an adjunct faculty member at Mercy College, where he teaches accounting and HR management in the master's degree program in HR management. Mr. Kreuter is the adviser to the student chapter of SHRM at Mercy College and is a member of SHRM's national research committee.

## Jonathan S. Monat, PhD, SPHR

Jonathan Monat is a professor of HR management at California State University in Long Beach. He received his PhD in Industrial Relations from the University of Minnesota, his MS in Employee Relations from San Diego State University, and his BS in Business Administration from UCLA. Dr. Monat's areas of expertise are labor relations, collective bargaining, dispute resolution, compensation, management of culture and diversity, strategic HR, and employment discrimination. His nonacademic experience includes labor arbitration, mediation, HR planning, and the design and implementation of compensation systems. As an active member of SHRM, Dr. Monat has served as chair of the national committee for college relations, as a member of the education committee, the education task force, and the research committee, and as a faculty adviser. Among the companies that Dr. Monat has consulted for are Westin International Hotels, Continental Airlines, Lummi Indian Tribal Enterprises, and McDonnell-Douglas.

## David Parent

As a manager of the Strategy Group for Deloitte & Touche, David Parent has served as the consulting project leader responsible for managing consultant activities and deliverables, project budgets and work plans, and client relations. He coordinated the initial user implementation, including testing, training, and problem resolution, for the initial rollout of PeopleSoft at three end-user locations. He also participated on a team responsible for relocating the entire benefits administration function of a major life insurance company, including health and welfare, pension, and 401(k) administration, from New York to a Michigan call center. Mr. Parent also established a quality control program, including call and case monitoring and customer satisfaction surveys, for a call center operation, and he reengineered the processes for billing various inactive employee populations for their benefits premiums. Mr. Parent's corporate clients have included a Fortune 100 telecommunications manufacturer, a Fortune 100 industrial conglomerate, health care systems in Michigan and Minnesota, and a leading global insurer. Mr. Parent has an MBA from the University of Michigan and a BS from the University of Illinois.

## Ellen R. Singer, EdD

Ellen Singer is a senior consultant with EMADJEN Management Consulting. She received a BA in 1970 from Hunter College, an MSEd in 1975 from James Madison University, and an EdD in 1995 from Vanderbilt University. Over the course of her career, Dr. Singer has worked as a technical writer, has been a director of HR and communications, and has taught organizational behavior and industrial psychology at James Madison University, Blue Ridge Community College, and Middle Tennessee State University. Her current research and publications focus on ethical issues, curriculum and instruction, and faculty development.

## Jeannette Swist, SPHR, CMC

Jeannette Swist is a principal consultant with Applied Resource Management. A Certified Management Consultant, she received an MS degree in Management and Organizational Behavior from George Williams College and has done postgraduate work in Organizational Development. Ms. Swist's prior experience includes building an HR management consulting practice for the seventh largest nationwide accounting, tax, and consulting firm, and for a management association. Both start-ups served client needs at the local, state, regional, and national level. Ms. Swist is an adjunct faculty member at National-Louis University, where she has taught HR, OB, and OD courses in the College of Management and Business for the past 12 years. She is an active member of many professional associations, including SHRM's national research committee.

## Daniel C. Wilson, EdD, SPHR

Daniel Wilson is the program head for the Human Resources/Business Administration program at Western Wisconsin Technical College (WWTC), where he has been teaching HR management and finance for more than 15 years. He established and continues to serve as the co-adviser for the WWTC student chapter of SHRM, the first technical college student chapter in the nation. He also serves as the student chapter liaison for the WWTC student chapter and the University of Wisconsin–La Crosse student chapter. Recently, Dr. Wilson taught HR in a doctoral program designed for international students. He became a member of SHRM in 1994 and earned the SPHR certification soon afterward. He co-authored a column on HR management for 2 years, and he has written numerous articles and made presentations at the state and national levels on a variety of HR issues. Dr. Wilson earned his EdD in Higher Education from Washington State University (1983), his MEd in Business Education from the University of Idaho (1979), and his BA in Economics from the University of Idaho (1973).

## Jennifer B. Wilson, PhD, SPHR

Jennifer Wilson has provided leadership as the executive director for human resources at the University of Wisconsin–La Crosse since the Office of Human Resources was created in 1994 as part of a universitywide strategic plan. Her prior work experience includes 4 years as assistant to the chancellor for affirmative action and 6 years as a psychologist (both at the University of Wisconsin–La Crosse); 4 years as a psychologist in private practice; and 2 years as a high school counselor. She also was an instructor of undergraduate and graduate courses at four universities (which included an HR management course to international doctoral students). Dr. Wilson co-authored an HR column for 2 years, she has 20 professional publications, and she has made more than 30 national and regional presentations. She has a PhD from Washington State University in Counseling Psychology (1983), an MEd from the University of Idaho in Guidance and Counseling (1979), and a BS from the University of Idaho in Psychology summa cum laude (1973). She was the 1997 recipient of the national SHRM Innovative Practice Award for a medium-sized company. Dr. Wilson's contribution to the profession through SHRM includes serving on the SHRM national research committee (since 1998), the innovative awards committee (1998), and the book award subcommittee (2000), writing a chapter for and co-editing this book; and writing and co-presenting the CCH/SHRM research on recruitment methods and sources at the 1999 annual conference. Dr. Wilson has been a member of the Wisconsin SHRM State Council, and she has served as a member of the board of directors, immediate past president, president, vice president, and chair of various committees for the La Crosse Area SHRM.

Chapter 1

# Research Methods: Investigation and Analysis

*Daniel G. Gallagher*

I n the course of performing their jobs, human resource (HR) professionals are frequently called on to exercise a broad range of technical and interpersonal skills. One such set of knowledge, skills, and abilities (KSAs), which can be central to the performance of the HR function and to the effectiveness of the employer organization, is the ability of the HR professional to undertake and successfully complete organizationally relevant research. In addition, the ability to critically evaluate the relevance and quality of research done by others, both within and outside the organization, is an important consideration associated with HR based changes in policy and practices.

For many people, the word "research" often conjures up the image of white-coated laboratory scientists testing new automobile designs in a wind tunnel or measuring the effectiveness of an experimental drug on the health of lab rats, or the image of a PhD candidate buried in a university library while studying the effects of the U.S. Civil War on the price of farmland. But in reality, research is a part of everyday life. Earl Babbie (1998) suggests that "science (physical and social) is an enterprise dedicated to *finding out*." In another sense, conducting research can be broadly viewed as a form of organizational *detective work*. Within the realm of human resource management (HRM), "finding out" or being an organizational detective is often a regular part of the job.

The goal of this chapter is to discuss some of the techniques or methods that can be used to find out the answers to issues or questions of concern to HR professionals and the organizations in which they work.

## Defining the Question

It is important to note that a starting point for good research is a clearly defined research question or questions. For Sherlock Holmes, the question might be straightforward, Who committed the crime? The medical scientist specifically wants to know, Does the newly developed drug significantly reduce blood pressure in adult men?

HR professionals should also start the research process with a clearly defined question or goal. Research questions may be (a) self-generated (e.g., I'm curious about the effect of the recently implemented _____ on _____), (b) generated from elsewhere in the organization (e.g., Why have overtime costs increased?), or (c) generated externally (e.g., Are you in compliance with court-ordered affirmative action orders?). The ability to research effectively and the way in which the research may be conducted are influenced by the specificity of the question or questions. A clear research question or purpose can greatly minimize the costs associated with HR-related research.

Not all research questions can be clearly defined at the outset, however. Good research questions can develop out of a sequential process. For example, take the issue of workforce turnover. The research should not start with the question, What should we do about employee turnover? but rather with the investigation of the following questions: (a) How much turnover do we have in our organization? (b) How does our turnover compare with the turnover in similar organizations in our type of industry? and (c) If the turnover it is excessive, what is the reason(s) for it? Those three questions give rise to three different research tasks: calculating turnover data, finding the industry or area average, and determining why people are leaving the organization. A finding that current turnover rates are actually below industry or area averages may preclude the need to address the related question, Why? Or the question could change to Why are people staying? An inquisitive HR professional might want to further specify the question and ask, Do average turnover rates underestimate the attrition rate for certain occupational groups?

## Purpose of the Research

The reason for conducting the research is as important as framing the research question(s). At one level, the purpose of research may be exploratory. Exploratory research may be undertaken to find out what an issue or HR practice or policy is about. For example, an HR professional might be interested in learning whether broad-banding (wider pay grades) would make a meaningful contribution to an organization's compensation system. As part of the initial exploration process, research could be directed toward collecting existing literature and expert opinions on the pros and cons of broad-banding. In addition, reading case studies of organizations that have undertaken broad-banding could elucidate the basics of such a compensation change. Exploratory research studies are typically conducted for three purposes: (a) to satisfy the researcher's curiosity or desire for a better understanding of the area of interest or concern, (b) to test the feasibility or need to undertake more extensive study, and (c) to develop the methods to be used in any subsequent study (Babbie, 1998).

Another purpose of research is to describe situations or events. The researcher observes or measures and then "describes" what was observed or measured. For example, on the basis of a review of government documents, an HR assistant might report annual national changes in the cost of living (COL) index over the past 10 years. Or a study of employees may find and report that 20% intend to leave the organization in the next 12 months. In many respects, descriptive research focuses on providing an account of the past or the current situation.

A third, and particularly sophisticated, purpose of research is to explain events, observations, or outcomes. Explanation goes beyond reporting what has occurred and moves into the domain of trying to understand why. For example, a researcher may find that 38% of employees are dissatisfied with the new profit-sharing plan and that women are more dissatisfied than men. The question that needs to be asked is obvious, or at least it should be obvious: Why are the employees dissatisfied? And why is dissatisfaction greater among women than men? In the context of explanation, the interest is in understanding why A leads to B or why one group's response is different from another's. Such a question opens the door to cause and effect and to the role of intervening variables or events.

## Types of Data and Measures

The analogy between detective work and HR research further suggests that the ability to effectively answer questions of interest depends on the ability to discover relevant evidence. In a broad sense, research focuses on measurement and interpretation. Measurement deals with the collection of information (e.g., facts, opinions, intentions, behaviors), and interpretation seeks to make sense out of the information.

Once the initial research question is framed (e.g., Are workers satisfied with the new employee involvement program?), attention needs to be directed toward selecting a method or methods for measuring or collecting relevant information. A variety of research methods or measurement techniques may be used. The selection of a measurement technique not only depends on the question being asked, but also requires consideration of the time and resources that are available to the HR investigator (Hollmann, 1994).

The various measurement or data collection techniques may be categorized into two broad dimensions. The first dimension is characterized by the extent to which the research method can be described as quantitative or qualitative. A second dimension or distinction, as noted in Figure 1–1, is based on the extent to which the investigation or research can be viewed as primary or secondary.

### Quantitative Versus Qualitative Approaches

Quantitative research methods generate numerical measures of the information that investigators seek to acquire in order to help answer questions of interest. Quantitative measures abound in everyday life. For example, the stock market is tracked by numerical changes in the Dow Jones or the New York Stock Exchange, unemployment is reported as a percentage of the labor force, and economic value or income is expressed in numerical currency values. Quantitative measures are very helpful in making distinctions about "more," "less," "the same," or "close to the same."

Qualitative research methods are more focused on the collection of information that either is difficult to quantify or should not be reduced to a numerical value in order to have meaning. For example, an organization that is interested in locating an office or a plant in a particular foreign country might want to investigate labor market conditions and a report providing descriptive quantitative data such as unemployment rates, average years of schooling, and wage and salary rates. However, equally valuable qualitative data is available through a review of national labor laws, a political profile of the country, and discussion with other foreign firms operating in the country of interest.

*Figure 1-1* _____

## A Typology of Data Sources and Methods

| | Quantitative | Qualitative |
|---|---|---|
| **Primary** | Primary Employee Surveys (scaled)<br>Field Experiments<br>Laboratory Experiments | Employee Surveys (open-ended)<br>Case Studies (internal)<br>Focus Groups<br>Interviews |
| **Secondary** | Secondary Organizational Archival Records<br>(e.g., turnover, absenteeism records)<br>Government Survey Data (e.g., BLS)<br>Industry Group and Consultant Surveys | Literature (i.e., books, journals, cases)<br>Historical Accounts<br>Legal Reports and Court Cases<br>Consulting and Private Reports<br>(e.g., generated by BNA, CCH, SHRM)<br>Employee Files |

It is also important to note that there is no clear basis to universally assume that quantitative research is better than qualitative research, or vice versa. The appropriateness of one method over the other depends on the questions being investigated and the resources that are available.

### Primary Versus Secondary Research

In many respects, the distinction between primary and secondary research is a question of ownership and control. Primary research can generally be characterized as information (data) collection that the researcher is directly responsible for gathering. In effect, the HR investigator (or the HR team) controls the methods that will produce the information that will be used to address questions of interest (e.g., How satisfied are employees with the recent changes in the employer's health care plan?). Primary research also tends to have a specific importance to the research questions under consideration.

In contrast, secondary research is characteristic of research that was initially conducted or gathered by other researchers or organizations. As noted in Figure 1–1, government data (unemployment rates, consumer price index, income and earnings reports) would be representative of secondary research material. Similarly, salary and benefit survey data collected by a consulting firm would typically constitute secondary information because the task of collecting the data is often outside the direct control of the HR researcher. It is also interesting to note that much internal organization data (e.g., old policy manuals, past performance evaluations, accident reports, attendance records) are normally characterized as secondary sources. Qualitative research may rely heavily on secondary research as a means of gathering information as part of an HR research project. Library searches that review academic and practitioner journals and that access court decisions via the Internet represent a form of qualitative research.

The appropriateness of primary or secondary data is a function of the question being asked. In fact, primary research may not be needed in situations in which others have already done the legwork (e.g., a literature review). In addition, secondary information (and qualitative data collection methods) may serve as the early phase of a multiphase investigation. The answer to the question Do we have a turnover problem? may come from archival or secondary data. The answer to the question Why are employees leaving? may be found through primary data collection.

## Data Collection Strategies and Methods

There is no ideal, best method for conducting organizational or HR-related research. The decision to use one strategy or another depends on a variety of factors, including the nature of the question or issue being researched, the purpose of the research, and both time and resource constraints. Furthermore, preliminary data collection may exist as a starting point for future research by helping identify which relevant factors to examine and which areas to investigate in more depth. Some of the data collection strategies that can be included in the HR research toolbox are described below.

## Archival or Historical Studies

From an HR perspective, understanding past experiences can greatly benefit the development of future courses of action or strategies. Archival or historical research often provides the HR researcher with a profile of past trends and experiences. Archival research is concerned with accumulating and organizing data from documents, records, and the testimony of participants and observers. Archival information can be either qualitative or quantitative. Many of the issues discussed in this handbook (e.g., employee turnover and absenteeism) can be examined through a review of existing files or historical records. Historical records in the form of organizational reports, policy manuals, and interviews with employees and managers can provide exploratory as well as descriptive accounts of past events and trends. Archival data are also helpful in providing a longitudinal record. With proper consideration of the role of intervening events (e.g., downsizing, computerization), historical data can also illuminate possible cause and effect relationships. Government surveys in the form of COL reports, unemployment data, employment figures, and earnings are a form of archival data.

## Literature Reviews

The foundation for effective HR research should include consideration of research that other individuals or organizations have done. In an early, exploratory stage, it may be instructive for HR professionals to review relevant literature before embarking on detailed or specific organizational research. Existing research may show the results of similar studies and may alert researchers to possible approaches and problems encountered by others in the study of similar issues (Hollmann, 1994). HR research is published in a wide range of professional and scholarly journals, including *HRMagazine, Academy of Management Executives, Academy of Management Journal, Human Resource Management, Human Resource Management Review, Industrial Relations, Journal of Applied Psychology, Journal of Organizational Behavior,* and *Public Personnel Management.*

Within the universe of existing literature are many beneficial external surveys and research reports executed by other organizations or individuals. Among the leading sources of external surveys and topical reports are the Bureau of National Affairs (BNA), the Commerce Clearing House (CCH), the U.S. Bureau of Labor Statistics, and professional organizations such as the Society for Human Resource Management (SHRM). Relevant background literature can be accessed on the Internet through a variety of search engines as well as specific site addresses (such as, <http://www.shrm.org/whitepapers> or <http://www.shrm.org/hrnews>).

## Case Studies

Case studies represent an approach to investigations that falls under the broader title of field research. For the most part, case studies focus on in-depth analysis of a single organization or unit within an organization. Case studies are often undertaken to describe and understand the impact of a potentially significant organizational event. For example, investigators (i.e., HR researchers) may be interested in acquiring detailed information concerning what, if any, impact the outsourcing of HR tasks may have on organizational performance. Ideally, case studies are designed to allow the investigator to collect data as the process or event unfolds. Above all, a case study should provide an understanding of what existed before the event (e.g., outsourcing), how the event was implemented, and what outcomes were produced. A major purpose of a case study is to provide a rich and detailed description of what has already occurred. However, case studies can also seek to explain the reasons for observed outcomes.

Participant observer–based research is a type of case study in which the researcher goes beyond the role of observing and chronicling events. That type of research also relies on the researcher's insights from having actively participated in the event. In many respects, the researcher is a day-to-day participant in the process or experience that is under examination.

Case-based research has many advantages in terms of the amount of detail and firsthand knowledge that it can generate for an organization. The approach is often limited, though, by the extent to which the data and findings can be generalized or applied to other organizations. The richness of case data can also help other researchers understand what to consider in the formulation of case-based studies or experiences within their own organizations.

## Surveys

As a measurement technique, surveys can serve a number of objectives. HR professionals can conduct internal surveys to assess the opinions, attitudes, and intended behaviors of employees (and management) within an organization. A common example of an internal questionnaire survey would be a general employee satisfaction survey. Other surveys might investigate a specific question such as the opinions of employees toward a new compensation plan, changes in the way annual performance appraisals are conducted, or organizational commitment. (For a detailed summary of survey-based scales, including scales on satisfaction, stress, justice, and communication, see Price, 1997.) Internal surveys can be used to measure or poll employee opinions and attitudes (e.g., 72% of the workers at the headquarters office are satisfied with the shift to a health maintenance organization medical delivery plan).

Survey data can also be used for *analytical* purposes (Hollmann, 1994). For example, information collected through a survey can be subjected to statistical analysis to determine if response differences (opinion, attitudes, etc.) exist on the basis of such factors as gender, age, tenure, or other individual or organizational characteristics.

A common inclination exists to incorrectly equate surveys with quantitative measurement. The tendency to quantify is often a result of the ability to translate survey responses into numerical values (e.g., strongly agree = 5, strongly disagree = 1, or male = 0, female = 1, etc.) thereby subjecting the responses to statistical analyses (correlations, comparisons of mean values). Although responses to questionnaires can be quantified (and the larger the sample, the greater the temptation to do so), questionnaire surveys can also be designed to focus on the collection of less quantifiable information. Questionnaire surveys can and often should contain open-ended questions such as Why do you feel this way? or What other factors may have influenced your feelings toward the new merit pay plan? Open-ended questions often yield useful qualitative data that provide insights into the reasons people hold certain opinions, allow survey participants to participate more actively in a survey, and often bring to the attention of the HR researchers issues or concerns that may have otherwise been overlooked because of survey design.

Surveys can be used to gather information on the HRM practices and policies of other organizations (e.g., wage and benefit surveys). Such external surveys can be conducted by HR practitioners, but large-scale projects are more likely to be carried out by such organizations as SHRM, CCH, or BNA. External survey data may hold particular value in assisting HR professionals in benchmarking the status of programs and policies within their own organization.

The collection of data through surveys is often associated with pencil-and-paper questionnaires or instruments. There has recently been considerable

growth in the use of electronic or computerized self-administered questionnaires (CSAQs). Under computerized data collection strategies, the subject
receives the survey instrument via electronic bulletin boards or other Internet
linkages. Such techniques allow an electronic response file to be automatically
created, hence reducing the need for subsequent data entry.

## Interviews

Valuable research or survey data can also be gathered through face-to-face
interviews with employees. Interview formats can range from extremely structured (i.e., precise predetermined questions are asked of all subjects in the same
order) to more nonstructured (e.g., "Tell me about your experiences with the
new employee involvement program."). Structured interview questions are especially important because they allow for a comparison of different responses to
the *same* research questions. Like written surveys, all interviews should allow
respondents at some point to provide comments and opinions about issues of
concern that may not have been specifically included on the list of predetermined questions. Likewise, interviewers should have the opportunity to ask for
an elaboration or explanation of an interviewee's responses. Interview methods,
like all other forms of data collection, also need to consider the issues of reliability and validity.

## Focus Groups

Focus groups, a traditionally popular technique for marketing research, have the
potential for allowing HR researchers to achieve a quick and detailed reaction of
employees to proposed or actual innovations. Focus groups, which typically con-
sist of 8 to 12 people, can often provide researchers with candid information
regarding employees' feelings about certain programs and suggestions for improvement. However, a disadvantage of focus groups is that, without proper training,
the focus group facilitator may lose group control or direction. In addition, the
variety of impressions may be difficult to analyze. Focus groups are a useful starting point in the task of determining the types of issues that an organization may
need to address in greater detail through other investigation strategies.

## Experiments

Experimental designs represent a more rigorous form of HR management
research. Well-constructed experimental designs can accurately assess cause and
effect (causality) and account for the effect of intervening variables, which may
have an impact on both outcomes and the interpretation of the experience.

For example, an HR researcher may be interested in determining if a flextime program can reduce absenteeism and increase job-related satisfaction. A useful experimental design to test the effect of the flextime program would create at least two groups of workers (who, ideally, would be randomly assigned). One group would be exposed to the "treatment" (i.e., flextime) and should be classified as the "experimental" group. The other group would continue its regular hours of work and would be classified as the "control" group. Measures of interest (e.g., absenteeism [via archival records] and job satisfaction [via survey]) would be made for both groups and administered before (pretest) and after (posttest) the treatment or intervention. The measures would then be compared for both groups over time (see Cook and Campbell, 1979). If there was a change in absenteeism and job satisfaction for the experimental group but not for the control group, the changes could be reasonably attributed to the implementation of the flextime program. Conversely, similar changes for both groups would suggest that a change is occurring but not necessarily as a result of the flextime program. Hollmann noted (1994) that experimental designs are frequently used to assess training programs or other developmental interventions.

## Managing and Interpreting Data

As suggested above, a range of sources and methods is associated with the collection of HR-related information. In many situations, interpreting information and findings may rely heavily on the experience and judgment of the researcher. But as the volume and complexity of available information expand, it may be useful for HR professionals to have access to technologies that can assist them in the generation, storage, retrieval, and analysis of information.

HR professionals should consider availing themselves of or investing in a Human Resource Information Systems (HRIS), which can be used to obtain and analyze data by means of the latest computer technology. For the task of quantitative data storage, analysis, and presentation, software applications such as Excel, or Statistical Package for the Social Sciences (SPSS) are illustrative of in-office or personal computer tools now normally accessible to most HR practitioners.

It is always important to consider the adage "Garbage in ... Garbage out." Regardless of how good the analytical technique is, poor-quality information can only lead to poor-quality results. Hence, the reliability and quality of data are prerequisites for quality results and interpretation.

Finally, HR professionals must be cautioned to avoid the temptation to over-interpret research or findings. "Causality" is one of the major errors in many research projects. In many cases, the absence of a time series or of longitudinal data constricts the researcher's ability to convincingly establish that A → B → C. If understanding causality is important, the researcher needs to take measurements at more than one point in time. For certain types of research, a cross-sectional snapshot of "what the situation is" may be sufficient. When conducting their research and interpreting the research of others, HR professionals should also be conscious of personal biases and of confusing "what is" with "what should be." Effective research focuses on the "what is" or "what has been." It is the task of other HR initiatives to make the changes to "what should be."

## Conclusion

Technological developments have put an increasingly accessible set of resources before HR professionals that can be used to measure and analyze data relevant to the effective delivery of organizational programs. When selecting a research strategy, the HR professional should always carefully consider two questions, regardless of the resources that are available: What are investigators trying to measure? and For what purposes are they seeking to use the information? Addressing those two basic questions can be a simple and helpful start to any HR research project.

## References and Suggested Readings

Babbie, E. (1998). *The practice of social research* (8th ed.). Belmont, CA: Wadsworth Publishing.

Bateman, T. S., & Ferris, G. R. (Eds.). (1984). *Methods and analysis in organizational research.* Reston, VA: Reston Publishing.

Cline, T. R. (1999). *Program assessment.* Reading, MA: Addison-Wesley.

Cook, J. D., & Campbell, D. T. (1979). *Quasi-experimental design and analysis for field settings.* Chicago: Rand-McNally.

Hollmann, R. W. (1994). HRD/D research. In W. R. Tracey, *Human resources management & development handbook* (2nd ed., pp. 381–396). New York: AMACOM.

Marshall, C., & Rossman, G. B. (1989). *Designing qualitative research*. Newbury Park, CA: Sage.

Miller, D. C. (1991). *Handbook of research design and social measurement* (5th ed.). Newbury Park, CA: Sage.

Price, J. L. (1997) Handbook of organizational measurement. *International Journal of Manpower, 18* (4,5,6).

Schmitt, N. W., & Klimoski, R. J. (1991). *Research methods in human resources management*. Cincinnati, OH: South-Western Publishing.

Schwab, D. P. (1999). *Research methods for organizational studies*. Mahwah, NJ: Lawrence Erlbaum Associates.

# Chapter 2

# Ethical Issues in HR Research

*Ellen R. Singer*

**H**uman resource (HR) practitioners are, by the very nature of their work, researchers. They employ research informally as well as systematically in order to understand, manage, and enrich the environments of employees and organizations. Major HR functions such as strategic planning, job analysis, job evaluation, selection and placement, performance appraisal, and training involve the use of analytical skills. Efforts directed at assessing HR effectiveness, such as HR audits, also fall within the domain of HR research. An operative knowledge of research techniques allows HR personnel to ask intelligent questions, aggregate and analyze data appropriately, make informed decisions, solve problems, and plan for future contingencies. In other words, "research on personnel management activities provides an understanding of what works, what does not work, and what needs to be done" (Mathis & Jackson, 1985, p. 527).

Before the 1960s, ethical discussions among researchers were rare, and behaviors now viewed as unconscionable (e.g., privacy and confidentiality violations) were acceptable and commonplace (Kimmel, 1996). Today, ethical issues compose a major component of research training and practice. Therefore, the use of unprincipled means in the execution of research can no longer be condoned or justified by the scientific ends or the esoteric purposes of a particular inquiry. Although thoughtfully designed research methodology furnishes individuals and organizations with useful information, it must be ethically as well as methodologically sound to be worthwhile.

Because organizational research is a value-laden enterprise, HR practitioners encounter a variety of ethical issues as they negotiate the research process. In some instances, deciding whether to conduct an inquiry represents a moral dilemma (Kimmel, 1996). Practical research generally occurs in natural settings, where researchers have less control over individuals and circumstances. Therefore, variance among scientific principles, real working conditions, and multiple (and possibly conflicting) values, goals, and roles is virtually inevitable. As a result of ambiguity and ill-defined guidelines, ethical matters may sometimes be slighted, compromised, or overshadowed by pragmatic considerations or even bureaucratic influences. For example, HR's involvement in ethical decision making is sometimes influenced by obstacles such as the diminished status of HR in the organizational hierarchy (Petrick, 1992).

## Informed and Voluntary Consent

The principle of informed consent, as delineated in the Ethical Code of the American Psychological Association (1992), requires researchers to apprise potential participants about their role in a study. Such information includes the overall purpose of the research, how and why the individuals were selected, and the procedures that will be used. Furthermore, the code states that participants should be advised that they have the right to withdraw their consent at any time during the research process. Because organizational research frequently takes place in the field, it is especially important for individuals to understand that a decision to enlist, decline, or withdraw from a research project will not affect their job outcomes. Although informed consent cannot always be obtained, researchers should routinely pursue this ideal. Researchers who employ that practice respect and protect the rights of individuals by affording them autonomy and the opportunity to make discerning choices concerning their participation.

Informed and voluntary consent may be obtained in various ways. For example, when the HR practitioner is conducting survey research, a short introduction explaining the nature and purpose of the research should be included in the survey. The consent of potential participants is confirmed or denied on the basis of whether or not they complete the survey. The introduction should also assure participants that their responses will be kept confidential and separate from other personnel information. Figure 2–1 illustrates a sample questionnaire introduction.

Figure 2–2 is an example of a consent form that could be used to secure an individual's permission to be interviewed for a research project. Under such circumstances, the interviewer should code all interview notes so that they cannot be connected to the interviewee at a later time. If the researcher uses this format, the participant's signed permission is requested.

*Figure 2-1*

## Sample Questionnaire Introduction

Dear Employee,

The HR department is conducting research about employee attitudes toward a new scheduling policy. The purpose of this questionnaire is to give you an opportunity to tell how you feel about this policy. Please try to answer every question. Your answers to all of the questions will be coded anonymously and they will in no way have anything to do with how your work performance is evaluated.

Thank you for your cooperation.

*Figure 2-2*

## Sample Consent Form

You are invited to participate in a research study conducted by the HR department to explore how employees feel about a new scheduling policy. You will be asked questions about the current and the new policies. Your participation in this study will require an interview of approximately one-half hour, which will be audiotaped.

Please understand that your participation in this study is voluntary. You have the right to refuse to answer particular questions, or you may withdraw your consent or discontinue your participation at any time without penalty. In addition, your individual privacy will be maintained in all published and written materials resulting from this study. The information will not be shared with any of your supervisors or managers and will have nothing to do with how your work performance is evaluated.

Thank you for your cooperation.

Signed _____     Date _____

## Privacy Issues

Communicating scientific knowledge deals with such issues as reporting results, sharing data, and plagiarism (American Psychological Association, 1992). It is self-evident that falsification and misrepresentation of data breach the ethical code of research conduct. A component of this ethical challenge involves ensuring the privacy of employees, clients, or organizations engaged in the research process. "The right to privacy may be looked upon as the right of the individual to decide the extent to which attitudes, opinions, behaviors, and personal facts will be shared with others" (Stone, 1978, p. 147). Because information obtained during the research process is confidential, ethical practices oblige investigators to treat research data and outcomes judiciously and confidentially. In addition, protecting the privacy rights of individuals extends to follow-up studies at a later time. However, the confidentiality ethic does not include participants in a study who have a prior understanding that the results will be shared with others. With the participant's consent, the researcher may ethically disclose information to others or use the information in supplemental formats such as reports or presentations.

Specific research procedures are available to safeguard the anonymity and confidentiality of individuals and institutions. Ideally, questionnaires should be designed so that participants may respond anonymously, thereby eliminating the need to code the responses. However, if complete anonymity cannot be realized, questionnaires may be coded blindly so that it is not feasible for specific institutions or respondents to be connected to the data. Gathering data in this manner not only secures the privacy of the survey participants, but also increases the probability that individuals will be willing to participate in the study. Furthermore, respondents are more likely to provide truthful responses, especially to sensitive questions, if their privacy is protected. Because blind coding enhances the accuracy of the data collected, this method renders a functional as well as an ethical purpose for HR professionals.

Ensuring privacy applies to the daily HR enterprise as well as to planned research activities. For example, decisions concerning the acquisition and dissemination of information in employee records are ethical dilemmas that frequently confront HR personnel. State laws and company policies differ in regard to the accessibility and use of information in personnel records, and those differences can heighten ethical considerations. Complete anonymity is sometimes infeasible. In circumstances where private information is inappropriately managed or carelessly handled, the potential for unethical behavior escalates.

Organizational policies that facilitate employee confidentiality may minimize ethical dilemmas. For example, an HR protocol may be initiated to restrict the access of employee records to appropriate personnel on a need basis only. Such a protocol, monitored by a "guardian of the records," might include the following information: the names of the individuals requesting and releasing the record, the date of the record's release and return, and the purpose of the request. A specified time period for retaining the record may be included as part of this practice. The additional red tape may discourage individuals from making unnecessary requests for records—a supplemental and favorable outcome of a more restrictive policy.

Additional techniques that address both research and practical issues may further promote the ethic of employee confidentiality. These techniques include the following:

- Interpreting research findings and other data on employees objectively rather than subjectively
- Reporting research findings in general rather than specific terms
- Destroying research data or other employee information that is are no longer necessary or legally required
- Archiving and preserving identifying information (i.e., names, social security numbers) under confidentiality conditions
- Keeping different kinds of records separate (e.g., medical and performance review)
- Divulging only necessary information rather than complete files
- Training HR personnel to treat employee information prudently

It is important to note that those practices should address follow-up circumstances as well as present conditions (Kimmel, 1988). For example, the possibility that the data may be used at a later date can be included in the informed consent procedure (Campbell & Kimmel, 1985).

## Resolving Ethical Dilemmas

Decision making may not always comply with scientific truths or reflect the most rational courses of action. Because ethical dilemmas are inevitable realities of organizational research, HR professionals should be highly sensitive to the personal, academic, practical, and legal implications of those dilemmas. Ethical dilemmas are difficult to resolve primarily because individuals (including researchers) and circumstances are subjective, complex, variable, and ambiguous. In instances where ethical issues must be settled singularly, decision making becomes even more burdensome. Although the legal system is open to interpretation and revision, it still offers HR practitioners a concrete framework to guide some of their decision making during the research process. For example, questions such as What makes an employment test valid? or Why is a selection technique discriminatory? may be settled in a court of law. However, ethical decisions that do not have the benefit of legal parameters or precedents are more difficult to reconcile. Confronted by equivocal guidelines and obscure issues, individuals frequently make decisions on the basis of personal standards. That strategy may cause attitudinal and behavioral inconsistencies because of variations across individuals' value systems. For example, the use of deception in a research study is viewed by some methodologists as legitimate under certain circumstances and by others as unethical under any conditions (Stone, 1978).

Reconciling ethical dilemmas may be facilitated to some degree by consulting federal and state regulations, codes of research ethics, and internal or external research committees and review boards. Numerous organizations, including the American Psychological Association, have issued such codes. Additional codes are cited in the references and suggested readings section to this chapter. Although the Society of Human Resource Management (SHRM) Code of Ethics (1994–1997) does not specifically target organizational research, one of its tenets clearly promotes the ethic of "maintaining confidentiality of privileged information" (p. 1). This ideology reverberates in codes of ethics across state and local SHRM chapters. During recent years, an international interest in ethical issues in psychological research has begun to emerge (Kimmel, 1996). Australia, Canada, France, Germany, and Spain are among the countries pursuing that interest.

Academicians and other professionals (i.e., attorneys and psychologists) can provide valuable resources to HR professionals engaged in research. For example, a human subjects research committee from a nearby college or university may be engaged to review a proposed project or to answer specific questions concerning research methodology. An organization or HR department may also form an ethics committee or a review board to assess the risks and benefits of conducting a study, to safeguard the rights of research participants, or to explore the ramifications of particular research methods and procedures. Sharing and rotating ethical decision-making responsibilities among HR personnel whenever feasible are beneficial practices. Such approaches not only expand the accountability for decision making, but also minimize the stress frequently associated with making ethical choices.

Various researchers (i.e., Rodriguez, 1992; Rosnow & Rosenthal, 1993) suggest approaches for ethically reviewing proposed research. For example, Rodriguez (1992) offers the Ethical Analysis Protocol as a reflective technique for self-analysis and peer review of research practices. Furthermore, the protocol provides researchers with an opportunity for ongoing ethical dialogue throughout the research process. The protocol focuses on three major areas: treatment of research participants, research practices, and sociopolitical dimensions. Rodriguez (1992) maintains that

> Consistent application of the protocol, the habit of asking relevant ethical questions of each research assignment [theoretical or practical], develops the ethical analysis skills of the researcher and provides additional assurance of the ethical credibility and integrity of one's research proposals, plans, and studies. (p. 57)

## Conclusion

Research contributes significantly to the theory and practice of HR management. A functional body of research knowledge provides HR professionals with scientific paradigms to interpret real-world phenomena and to solve real-world problems by engaging in more than trial and error–based solutions. However, the process of conducting HR research can also create an exacting enterprise fraught with difficult questions and conflicting methods. The professional response to this challenge must acknowledge from the onset that the difficulties inherent in HR research, realistic as they may be, do not justify unethical or slipshod research practices. For HR inquiry to be meaningful and practical, it must embrace both a human and a scientific ethic.

## References and Suggested Readings

Adair, J. G. (1988). Research on research ethics. *American Psychologist, 43*(10), 825–826.

American Psychological Association. (1974). *Standards for educational and psychological tests.* Washington, DC: Author.

American Psychological Association. (1981a). Ethical principles of psychologists. *American Psychologist, 36*(6), 633–638.

American Psychological Association. (1981b). Specialty guidelines for the delivery of services by industrial/organizational psychologists. *American Psychologist, 36*(6), 664–669.

American Psychological Association. (1992). *Ethical principles of psychologists and code of conduct* [On-line]. Available: <http://www.apa.org/ethics/code.html>.

Blanck, P. D., Bellack, A. S., Rosnow, R. L., & Rotheram-Borus, M. J. (1992). Scientific rewards and conflicts of ethical choices in human subjects research. *American Psychologist, 47*(7), 959–965.

Campbell, D. T., & Kimmel, A. J. (1985). *Guiding preventive intervention research centers for research validity.* Rockville, MD: Department of Health and Human Services.

Caplan, A. L., & Callahan, D. (Eds.). (1981). *Ethics in hard times.* Hastings-on-the-Hudson, NY: The Hastings Center, Institute of Society, Ethics, and the Life Sciences.

Grisso, T., Baldwin, E., Blanck, P. D., & Rotheram-Borus, M. J. (1991). Standards in research: APA's mechanism for monitoring the challenges. *American Psychologist, 46*(7), 758–766.

Kahn, W. A. (1990). Toward an agenda for business ethics research. *Academy of Management Review, 15*(2), 311–338.

Kimmel, A. J. (1988). *Ethics and values in applied social research.* Newbury Park, CA: Sage.

Kimmel, A. J. (1996). *Ethical issues in behavioral research.* Cambridge, MA: Blackwell.

Levine, R. J. (1975). *The nature and definition of informed consent in various research settings.* Paper prepared for the National Commission for the Protection of Human Subjects of Biomedical and Behavioral Research, Bethesda, MD: U.S. Department of Health, Education, and Welfare.

London, M., & Bray, D. W. (1980). Ethical issues in testing and evaluation for personnel decisions. *American Psychologist, 35*(10), 890–901.

Lowman, R. (1985). *Casebook on ethics and standards for the practice of psychology in organizations.* College Park, MD: Society for Industrial and Organizational Psychology.

Mathis, R. L., & Jackson, J. H. (1985). *Personnel human resource management* (4th ed.). St. Paul, MN: West Publishing.

Mirvis, P. H., & Seashore, S. E. (1979). Being ethical in organizational research. *American Psychologist, 34*(9), 766–780.

Petrick, J. A. (1992). Organizational ethics development and the human resource professional. *Journal of Career Planning and Employment, 52*(4), 71–76.

Randall, D. M., & Gibson, A. M. (1990). Methodology in business ethics research: A review and critical assessment. *Journal of Business Ethics, 9*(6), 457–471.

Rodriguez, R. G. (1992). The ethical analysis protocol. In M. E. Schlitz (Ed.), *Ethics and standards in institutional research* (pp. 57–66). San Francisco: Jossey-Bass.

Rosnow, R. L., & Rosenthal, R. (1993). *Beginning behavioral research: A conceptual primer.* New York: MacMillan.

Schlitz, M. E. (Ed.). (1992). *Ethics and standards in institutional research.* San Francisco: Jossey-Bass.

Schrader-Frechette, K. S. (1994). *Ethics of scientific research.* Lanham, MD: Rowman & Littlefield.

SHRM Foundation. (1994–1997). *Mission statement and code of ethics* [On-line]. Available: <http://www.shrm.org/docs/ethics.htm>.

Sieber, J. E. (1977). What is meant by ethics? *American Psychologist, 32*(8), 684–685.

Sieber, J. E. (1994). Will the new code help researchers to be more ethical? Special section: The 1992 ethics codes: Boon or bane? *Professional Psychology Research and Practice, 25*(4), 369–375.

Society for Industrial and Organizational Psychology, Inc. (1987). *Principles for the validation and use of personnel selection procedures* (3rd ed.). College Park, MD: Author.

Stone, E. F. (1978). *Research methods in organizational behavior.* Santa Monica, CA: Goodyear Publishing.

## Chapter 3

# Job Analysis and Selection: Validity and Reliability

*Jeffrey R. Hoffmann*

J ob analysis and selection methods are the foundation for assessing and ful-filling the personnel needs of an organization. Job analysis is the first step in defining the tasks to be performed, the context of the work, and the human attributes required to perform the work. A well-planned job analysis forms the basis for developing selection procedures used to predict job per-formance and to provide the best fit between employee and organization.

The legal requirements for job analysis and employee selection are defined in the *Uniform Guidelines on Employee Selection Procedures* (EEOC, 1978). The two professional standards that are frequently cited in the *Uniform Guidelines*, and upon which both human resource (HR) professionals and the courts rely, are the *Standards for Educational and Psychological Testing* (AERA, APA, NCME, 1985) and the *Principles for the Validation and Use of Personnel Selection Proce-dures* (SIOP, 1987).

To conduct an effective job analysis, one must understand the target job within the context of the needs of the organization. With extensive use of com-puters and greatly improved communications during the last quarter century, the resulting trend toward "flattening" of traditional organizational hierarchies has reduced the ranks of middle management and subsequently shifted many tasks to other employees. This trend has markedly changed four dimensions of work: (a) increased employee decision making, (b) broader scope of tasks, (c) increased cognitive complexity of tasks, and (d) increased need for social inter-actions with other employees, customers and suppliers (CTEHP, 1999). The once clear distinctions between traditional blue-collar workers and white-collar managers have been blurred. Secretaries, previously limited to typing and filing, have had their responsibilities expanded to include administrative functions. Home appliance technicians have added the tasks of estimating, billing, and sales to their basic technical responsibilities. As the division between traditional job categories has faded, the role of the job analyst has become more critical and considerably more complex. If the true nature of a job's required knowledge, skills, abilities, and other characteristics (KSAO) are to be ascertained, the analyst must appreciate the scope of the job and avoid preconceived beliefs about the content of a job on the basis of existing job titles or descriptions. The examination of recent trends in work and the implications of those trends for job analysis can be found in *The Changing Nature of Work: Implications for Occupational Analysis* (CTEHP, 1999), *Enhancing Organizational Performance* (Druckman, Singer, & Van Cott, 1997), and *The Work of Nations: Preparing Ourselves for 21st-Century Capitalism* (Reich, 1992).

There are two steps involved in conducting any job analysis. First is the task-oriented or job-oriented analysis, which identifies the important tasks and behaviors necessary to perform the work. The second step is the worker-oriented analysis, which identifies the KSAO necessary to successfully carry out the tasks identified in the first step.

## Task-Oriented Analysis

The first step of job analysis is the identification of the important job requirements, including the tasks, duties, responsibilities, and performance standards. This information can be gathered through interviews with job incumbents or supervisors, the observation of workers, or the examination of archived documents such as written procedures, position descriptions, and training manuals. Direct observation of performance is most appropriate for manual or standardized jobs in which the job analyst can expect to witness the majority of important job tasks and behaviors within a reasonable period of time. Direct observation is not appropriate when there are great variations in activities from day to day, when critical situations arise only periodically, or when the job involves a great deal of mental activity (as in computer programming or accounting). In such cases, interviews of job incumbents or supervisors can be effective because those individuals may be able to describe any nonroutine tasks or activities that would not normally be observed by a job analyst. In all cases, it is necessary to identify both the importance of the task to the outcome of the work and the frequency with which the tasks occurs.

## Worker-Oriented Analysis

Once the important aspects of a job have been identified, the next step is to determine what it will take to accomplish the work in a satisfactory manner.

The worker-oriented analysis identifies or implies the KSAO necessary to perform the previously identified tasks. Knowledge is the specific information needed to perform a job, and knowledge is gained through experience and formal training. Examples are knowledge of welding procedures, knowledge of a word processing program, or knowledge of a building code. Skills are observable competencies or proficiencies needed to perform a function or a task. Examples are skill at welding, word processing, or operating a truck. Skills are normally acquired through practice and, like knowledge, can be improved on the job or through formal training. Skills usually have physical and cognitive components. The skill for typing, for example, involves eye-hand coordination and mental processing facility. Abilities are the competencies needed to perform the required job skills, and abilities often represent an individual's maximum potential to develop certain knowledge. Abilities, which may be physical or cognitive, are considered relatively stable over time. Examples are the ability to perform math functions, recall a list of numbers accurately, or climb a telephone pole. The category of other characteristics includes aspects of personality, interests, and physical or mental tolerance of stress. It is important to recognize that knowledge and skills, though desirable in an applicant, may not be critical because they can be developed with experience and training. Abilities and other characteristics represent an individual's potential for improving the knowledge and skills brought to the job.

The acronym KSAO is often misused as if it were a single concept. However, when an HR practitioner performs a job analysis, it is appropriate to consider KS and AO separately (Harvey, 1991). The distinction between KS and AO in job analysis will help clarify the inferences made between tasks and behaviors and the inferred KSs and AOs. In terms of job analysis, KSs are observable or readily defined, whereas AOs are generally inferred. In terms of selection, KSs can be developed and improved, whereas AOs represent the potential of the applicant. Therefore, the abilities and other characteristics that an applicant possesses represent the potential to acquire knowledge and develop skills; they are what make individuals unique (Harvey, 1991).

## Job Analysis Tools

Commercially developed tools are available to aid in the identification of job requirements. One such tool is the Position Analysis Questionnaire (PAQ). The PAQ and similar tools are known as deductive methods because they start with existing job taxonomies that have been developed from the analysis of thousands of jobs over many years. Those taxonomies contain hundreds of job descriptions in terms of tasks and associated KSAOs. Deductive methods are most appropriate for analyses involving a large number of jobs or when a job is not so unique as to defy all forms of categorization. Such a method is limited because it assumes the job being analyzed is comparable to some previously analyzed job. The PAQ is a frequently used questionnaire containing 195 items that describe worker-oriented job elements, including information input, work output, mental processes, relationships with other people, and job context. The result of the PAQ provides the basis for inferring KSAO and for comparing the results to analyses of similar jobs. Other inventories include the Functional Job Analysis, the Fleishman Job Analysis Surveys, and the Common Metric Questionnaire. Commercially developed inventories and questionnaires are available for both general use and specific types of jobs (e.g., machinist, secretary, or manager). A review of 20 such methods and instruments can be found in Whetzel and Wheaton (1997).

Of all the developments in job analysis, none is as revolutionary as the Occupational Information Network (O*NET). The O*NET, developed by the U.S. Department of Labor over several years, is a comprehensive database of worker attributes and job characteristics that was designed to replace the Dictionary of Occupational Titles (DOT) by the end of 2000. The development of O*NET was driven by the recognition that the U.S. workforce is evolving from predominantly task-based blue-collar workers to multifaceted, skills-based workers (CTEHP, 1999; Mariani, 1999; Whetzel & Wheaton, 1997). The O*NET content model includes six categories. The first three categories describe worker-oriented requirements:

1. Worker requirements
    a. Skills
    b. Knowledge
    c. Education
2. Worker characteristics
    a. Abilities
    b. Interests
3. Experience requirements.

The remaining three categories describe job-oriented requirements:

4. Occupational requirements

a. Work activities

b. Context

c. Organizational context

5. Occupational-specific requirements

a. Tasks

b. Duties

c. Equipment

6. Occupational characteristics

a. Labor market information

b. Occupational outlook

c. Wages

The O\*NET98 software is available from the O\*NET Center at <http://www.onetcenter.org>.

When a job is unique and does not fit one or more previously defined job categories, or when there is reason to perform a job analysis "from scratch," inductive job analysis methods may be better suited. Inductive job analysis methods start with listing detailed information about the tasks and what is needed to perform the work. The lists are then categorized and ranked in terms of their importance to some outcome and frequency of occurrence. From this prioritized ranking, the most important KSAOs needed to perform the work can be identified. The consequences of certain behaviors, or lack thereof, may result in negative outcomes in certain jobs. That situation might be the case for airline pilots, nurses, construction workers, or even accountants. In such cases, rating of the behaviors that may lead to or avoid significant errors will also be useful in identifying which KSAOs may be more important to successfully performing a job.

The Critical Incident Method, the best-known inductive method, involves the collection of anecdotes that describe job-related situations in terms of what led to the incident, the context of the situation, a description of the employee's behaviors, and the consequences of those behaviors. The incident may have either a positive or negative outcome, provided that the outcome is critical or significant. In all cases, the incident must have been influenced one way or another by the employee. Though more involved than can be described here, the critical incidents are categorized and ranked, and from those actions the KSAOs can be inferred. One limitation of the critical incident method is that it is time consuming; several hundred incidents may be required for a thorough job analysis of relatively complex jobs.

*Figure 3-1*

## Job Analysis Validation

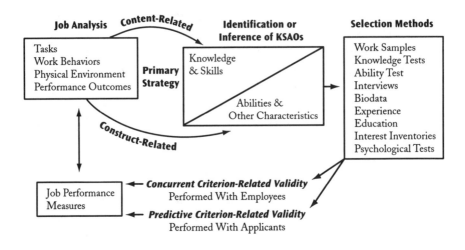

## Validity

Validity is the measure of the accuracy of a selection test or the measure for predicting job performance. Validity is not inherent in any test but indicates how appropriate the test is for a particular use. Validation of job analysis and selection procedures is required by the Equal Employment Opportunity Commission (EEOC) and is often the foundation on which discrimination and adverse impact suits are based. Four types of validity are important to job analysis: concurrent criterion-related validity, predictive criterion-related validity, content-related validity, and construct-related validity. Figure 3–1 shows the relationship between job analysis, inferences made concerning KSAOs, selection method, and validation.

Criterion-related validity is the relationship between a selection procedure score (predictor) and a measure of job performance or behaviors (criterion). The focus here is not the test scores themselves, but how they correlate with the criterion (hence the name). As long as the predictor is significantly correlated with the job performance, any attempts to explain the relationship are relatively unimportant (Cascio, 1997). For selection purposes, criterion-related validity is compelling both for hiring and in the courts if challenged. Predictors may include ability tests, work samples, interview ratings, personality inventories, or ratings of experience. For example, a math test can be considered to have high criterion-related validity if it correlates positively with the job performance of a bank teller.

Concurrent criterion-related validity measures the correlation between employee performance and employee test scores, both of which are measured at approximately the same time. An example of this type of validity would involve the administration of a dexterity test to circuit board assemblers and the measurement of their performance in terms of speed and accuracy of board assembly. A high correlation would indicate that the dexterity test measures something important for this job. The limitation of concurrent criterion-related validity is in using the same test to predict performance of job applicants. Concurrent validity is often used in place of predictive validity, at least initially, because of the impracticality of hiring all applicants who are tested. If a concurrent criterion-related test will be used to predict future performance of job applicants, inferences have to be made concerning potential differences between present employee performance and test scores. For example, it can be expected that the test scores of existing employees will be higher and less variable than the scores of job applicants. This scenario is especially true when the test measures knowledge or skills that may have been learned or improved on the job. This potential lack of variability in employee test scores is known as restriction in range of the criterion that, if present, would produce an artificially lowered validity coefficient compared to the results obtained if the entire pool of job applicants were tested. To some extent, restriction in range of the criterion can be compensated for statistically (Whetzel & Wheaton, 1997).

Predictive criterion-related validity is the correlation between test scores and future job performance. Because it is not likely that all applicants will be hired after being administered a selection test, either a top-down selection from ranking the applicants' scores or a cut-off score must be imposed to limit the number of hires. Because the rejected applicant's job performance will not be known, only those applicants selected will have their scores correlated with job performance. This situation again presents the problem of restriction in range of the predictor measure, which will result in the underestimation of the validity coefficient.

Content-related validity is the extent to which a selection method represents some portion of the behaviors being assessed. Content-related validity does not involve correlation coefficients but is determined by subject matter experts (SMEs), who decide the extent to which a predictor samples the domain of work behaviors. In this sense, content-related measures involving specific knowledge and skills are interchangeable with the job tasks. Tests of relevant job knowledge, proficiency tests, and work samples may be used as part of a content-related validity study. For example, a work sample consisting of word processing knowledge will have high content-related validity if word processing constitutes a significant portion of the job. Likewise, a paper-and-pencil test on knowledge of general chemistry and safe chemical handling will have high content validity when given to technicians who have applied for work in a chemical laboratory.

Construct-related validity is most appropriate for testing psychological constructs, including personality characteristics, conscientiousness, motivation, spatial relations, and math ability. Constructs are used to explain behaviors that are not directly observable. For example, outgoing behavior is not a construct, whereas extroversion is. To develop a new selection method based on the construct "conscientiousness," the researcher would have to determine if the test that supposedly measures conscientiousness is measuring something unique or if it is measuring some other construct such as honesty or integrity. There are two aspects to construct-related validity. The proposed construct should have convergent validity or should correlate with measures of similar constructs. The proposed construct should also possess divergent validity or should have little or no correlation with dissimilar constructs. Construct-related validity is the only form of validity that actually attempts to explain the relationship between the predictor and the criterion and that is therefore considered the ultimate criterion (Cascio, 1997; Harvey, 1991).

## Reliability of Job Analysis Information

Reliability is the extent to which a measure is consistent or stable. The four forms of reliability of interest to job analysis are interrater reliability, rate-rerate reliability, internal consistency, and the standard error of measurement. Interrater reliability is the degree to which rating scores agree between two or more job analysts, job incumbents, supervisors, or others completing a job analysis questionnaire or inventory. Inconsistencies represent either true variance in scores or differences in how items are responded to by different individuals (which is error variance).

Rate-rerate reliability is a measure of the consistency of job analysis measurements over time. Assuming there is no reason for any change in the job characteristic being measured, any change can be considered error variance. Depending on the job, the time limit may range from weeks to years before there is significant change in the content of the job.

Internal consistency is the measure of reliability of a job analysis instrument. Instruments that contain multiple items that sample a specific component of work should provide the responses. This form of reliability is normally applied only to job analysis instruments that contain many descriptors of the same task or behavior.

The standard error of measurement (SEM) establishes a range or confidence band around a true score. In job analysis the SEM can be used to differentiate between test scores for different groups or different jobs. Defining a range of scores around a hypothetical "true" score SEM helps prevent the problem of attributing more significance to a score than it may actually possess. The formula for the SEM follows:

$$\sigma_{measure} = \sigma_x \sqrt{(1-r_{xx})}$$

where $\sigma_{measure}$ is the SEM
$\sigma_x$ is the standard deviation of scores
$r_{xx}$ is the reliability
(Cascio, 1997; Harvey, 1991).

## Selection

After the job analysis has been completed, the next task is the identification of a selection method that will reflect the required KSAOs. Selection methods can range from commercially developed ability and personality tests to tests developed in house, work samples, and even interviews. Commercially developed tests are big business and should be approached with this in mind. Certain tests such as handwriting analysis, which supposedly measures various aspects of personality, have been shown to have no significant criterion-related validity with any aspect of job performance and no construct-related validity with any aspect of personality (Schmidt & Hunter, 1998). The fact that handwriting analysis is widely used as a selection test in Europe and to some extent in the United States (Ben-Shakhar, Bar-Hillel, Bilue, Ben-Abba, & Flug, 1986; Schmidt & Hunter, 1998) does not mean it is a valid test according to the EEOC (1978); AERA, APA, and NCME (1985); or SIOP (1987). Over the years, many tests and theories of human measurement have been proposed that are less obvious in their shortcomings (Gould, 1981) but should be approached with equal skepticism. Ultimately, it is the responsibility of the test administrator to use good judgment in seeking a reliable and valid test. Section 1607.9 of the *Uniform Guidelines on Employee Selection Procedures* (EEOC, 1978) is very clear on this point.

Under no circumstances will the general reputation of a test or other selection procedures, its author or its publisher, or casual reports of its validity be accepted in lieu of evidence of validity. Specifically ruled out are: assumptions of validity based on a procedure's name or descriptive labels; all forms of promotional literature; data bearing on the frequency of a procedure's usage; testimonial statements and credentials of sellers, users, or consultants; and other non-empirical or anecdotal accounts of selection practices or selection outcomes.

A number of references are available that can provide the HR professional with information concerning the appropriate uses of commercially available tests, including validity and reliability information. Sources of information concerning appropriate test use (including reliability and validity) appear in the reference section.

## Conclusion

Few issues are as important to an organization or have as lasting an impact as hiring the most qualified people for a particular job. Too often underrated, job analysis is the first step toward fulfilling that goal. Managers and job candidates alike may be more confident in the potential for acceptable performance and good fit within the organization when the hiring process follows a quality job analysis. Job analysis and validation of selection methods are not goals in themselves but two aspects of a never-ending sequence of refining organizational performance. As the 21st century gets under way, organizations, work, and employee requirements can be expected to continue to evolve. Job analysis is an effective tool for understanding and adapting to these changes.

## References and Suggested Readings

American Educational Research Association, American Psychological Association, & National Council on Measurements in Education. (1985). *Standards for education and psychological testing.* Washington, DC: Author.

American Psychological Association. (1998). *The ethical practice of psychology in organizations.* Washington, DC: Author.

American Psychological Association. (1999). *Frequently asked questions on psychological tests* [On-line]. Available: <http://www.aoa.org/science/test.html>.

Ben-Shakhar, G., Bar-Hillel, M., Bilue, Y., Ben-Abba, E., & Flug, A. (1986). Can graphology predict occupational success? Two empirical studies and some methodological ruminations. *Journal of Applied Psychology, 71*, 645–653.

Buros Institute of Mental Measurements, University of Nebraska, Lincoln, NE. [On-line]. Available: <http://www.unl.edu.buros>.

Cascio, W. F. (1997). *Applied psychology in human resource management* (5th ed.). Englewood Cliffs, NJ: Prentice-Hall.

Committee on Techniques for the Enhancement of Human Performance: Occupational Analysis, Commission on Behavioral and Social Sciences and Education, National Research Council. (1999). *The changing nature of work: Implications for occupational analysis.* Washington, DC: National Academy Press.

Druckman, D., Singer, J. E., & Van Cott, H. (Eds.). (1997). *Enhancing organizational performance.* Washington, D.C.: National Academy Press.

Equal Employment Opportunity Commission. (1978). *Uniform guidelines on employee selection procedures.* 29 CFR 1607.

Gould, S. J. (1981). *The mismeasure of man.* New York: W. W. Norton.

Guion, R. M. (1991). Personnel assessment, selection and placement. In M. D. Dunnette & L. M. Hough (Eds.), *Handbook of industrial and organizational psychology* (pp. 327–397). Palo Alto, CA: Consulting Psychologists Press.

Harvey, R. J. (1991). Job analysis. In M. D. Dunnette & L. M. Hough (Eds.), *Handbook of industrial and organizational psychology* (pp. 71–163). Palo Alto, CA: Consulting Psychologists Press.

Impara, J. C., & Murphy, L. L. (Eds.). (1995). *The 12th mental measurements yearbook.* Lincoln, NE: Buros Institute of Mental Measurements.

Keyser, D. J., & Sweetland, R. C. (Eds.). (1994). *Test critiques: Vol. 10.* Austin, TX: Pro-Ed.

Mariani, M. (1999, Spring). Replace with a database: O*NET replaces the dictionary of occupational titles. *Occupational Outlook Quarterly, 43,* 3.

Muchinksy, P. M. (1999). *Psychology applied to work: An introduction to industrial and organizational psychology* (6th ed.). Belmont, CA: Wadsworth/ Thompson Learning.

Murphy, L. L., Plake, B. S., & Impara, J. C. (Eds.). (1999). *Tests in print V: An index to tests, test reviews, and the literature on specific tests.* Lincoln, NE: Buros Institute of Mental Measurements.

National Academy Press (publishes books and articles by the various committees of the National Academy of Sciences, including the Committee on Techniques for the Enhancement of Human Performance) [On-line]. Available: <http://www.nap.edu>.

National O*NET Consortium (provides information about the Occupational Information Network and has FAQs, R&D issues, demos and products, including the O*NET Viewer Software [downloadable or available for purchase on CD]). [On-line]. Available: <http://www.onetcenter.org.practices>.

Position Analysis Questionnaire (PAQ) and the Professional and Managerial Position Questionnaire (PMPQ). [On-line]. Available: <http://www.paq.com>.

Reich, R. B. (1992). *The work of nations: preparing ourselves for 21st-century capitalism.* New York: Vintage Books.

Schmidt, F. L., & Hunter, J. E. (1998). The validity and utility of selection methods in personnel psychology: Practical and theoretical implications of 85 years of research findings. *Psychological Bulletin, 124*(2), 262–274.

Society for Industrial and Organizational Psychology. (1987). *Principles for the validation and use of personnel selection procedures* (3rd ed.). College Park, MD: Author.

Uniform Guidelines on Employee Selection Procedures. (1978). [On-line]. Available: <http://www.dol.gov/dol/esa/public/regs/cfr/41cfr/toc_chapt60/60_3_toc.htm>.

U.S. Department of Labor, Employment and Training Administration. (1999). *Testing and assessment: An employer's guide to good practices.* Washington, DC: Government Printing Office. [Also on-line]. Available: <http://www.doleta.gov/programs/onet/news.html>.

U.S. Department of Labor. (2000). *Occupational information network (O\*NET)* (the database of occupational descriptions that replaced the Dictionary of Occupational Titles [DOT]) in 2000). [On-line]. Available: <http://www.doleta.gov/programs/onet>.

U.S. Department of Labor Statistics. [On-line]. Available: <http://www.dls.gov>.

Whetzel, D. L., & Wheaton, G. R. (Eds.). (1997). *Applied measurement methods in industrial psychology.* Palo Alto, CA: Davies-Black Publishing.

## Chapter 4

# Measuring HR Value Through Benchmarking

### *Jeannette Swist*

enchmarking is action research. It is the process of identifying, discovering, learning, understanding, and evaluating key performance measures and of adapting practices, metrics, and processes across companies and industries. Benchmarking is one way to initiate and accelerate the change process, leading to "out-of-the-box" thinking while identifying change and targets for improvement. It provides a realistic viewpoint of strengths and limitations, of where the organization is today, and of what is and is not working. Benchmarking helps identify value-added improvement opportunities and insights that promote the need for change to top management.

## Step 1: Planning

Designing a benchmark involves a four-step process: plan, research, analyze, and implement.

The first phase of the planning process calls for an audit of human resource (HR) activities to identify which activities have been successful and which have not. The only way to decide is to document, measure, and analyze data. HR practice areas that may be audited include selection and placement, training and development, compensation, benefits, employee relations, health, and safety. Typical practice area measurements involve employee turnover, absenteeism, accidents, and employee attitudes. More often, organizations deal with issues by waiting until they hear a warning signal, or they find out what is not working when there is a crisis.

It is in an organization's best interests to undertake ongoing or periodic audits to measure effectiveness. A thorough audit consists of looking at HR activities and their effect across three levels: (a) day-to-day operations, (b) midlevel impact, and (c) strategic initiative implementation. An audit of only one of the three levels will provide a limited review. The day-to-day operational audit looks at the interactions, work processes, and standard operating procedures. A midlevel audit reviews decisions made at the managerial level and their effect on issues, service, policies, and practices. For instance, if the review is on the implementation of strategic initiatives, the resulting focus is on adaptation, transition, and change.

An organization should not overlook the importance of accurately assessing where it is today. Tracking results allows an organization to create internal benchmarks.

## Internal Benchmarking Opportunities

An audit of day-to-day operations looks at internal data collected by HR or related departments. Such a review identifies strengths or limitations in present policies, practices, and procedures. An audit of midlevel impact conducts interviews with key managers to get their ideas on current and desired HR practices and effects. The goal is to identify the gaps. An audit of strategic initiatives identifies how the strategic plan will affect HR. Key managers must be interviewed to determine how they think the plan will affect them. Brainstorming "what if" scenarios may be helpful.

Benchmarking provides choices. One choice is to look at what other organizations are doing. Often, organizations simply overlook key features or innovative developments already occurring within the organization. One form of internal benchmarking involves tracking data (e.g., turnover, employee attitudes, or customer service) over a designated period. An analysis of the data may show particular trends. Trend data provide a way to gauge progress, make continuous improvement, and plan for new programs and implementation of strategic initiatives.

## Employee and Customer Surveys

Employee surveys measure and benchmark the results of servicing internal customers, a company's employees, effectively and efficiently. For example, every other year for the past 10 years, a replacement parts distributor administered an organization survey to its employees. The survey results gave information to management (numbers, percentages, rankings, norms, and demographic breakouts for both items and categories of questions) to help the managers run the organization more effectively. Additionally, the survey results served as a benchmark. As each survey was completed, its measures became the basis of comparison. The surveys helped identify progress, trends, and perceived differences in the responses to each question, the category of questions, demographic groupings, and locations over time. It has been interesting to watch the individuals in top management use the survey results to benchmark themselves against their previous results. Top management uses the biennial survey results as an opportunity to work toward continuous improvement in employee satisfaction issues. From the results, top management forecasts a percentage increase; management then uses the results to see how closely the figures compare. A few examples of topics that the survey addressed follow:

- In the near future, I will probably look for a new job.
- I clearly understand the vision of my company.
- This company sees the value of offering employees a flexible work schedule.
- I have a complete understanding of how people advance in this organization.
- My contribution toward health insurance is fair.
- Participating in the upward appraisal of my supervisor is helpful to our business relationship.

Knowing employees' opinions and perceptions can help with making informed midlevel policy and strategic decisions. For example, the replacement parts distributor learned two important pieces of information: (a) a third of the company workforce is a "revolving door," and (b) a paradox exists in the company attendance policy and practices, thereby causing much upheaval and distress in the organization. Continual turnover of one third of the workforce has strategic implications. Management is investigating the problem. Management took swift and corrective action on the attendance policy by its serious consideration of employees' concerns and requested changes.

It is also possible to measure and benchmark the results of servicing customers. Over several years, a health care provider tried many programs to improve customer service. Those efforts included various training and recognition programs that were identified as "best practices." In spite of the effort, customer service scores remained in the low to average range. In the past year, a multidisciplinary committee of employees met and conducted many patient and employee interviews regarding customer service and developed service standards. Those service standards expressed the necessity of teamwork, focused on the customer experience, and were department specific. As the organization initiated the service standards, the multidisciplinary committee of employees required each department to have meetings. In the meetings, information was shared with employees that revealed department-specific survey results. The meeting format highlighted customer service expectations, standards, and measures, and it illustrated departmental strengths and developmental areas. The facilitators asked employees to contribute to the discussions and to write a personal commitment to deliver desired customer service that will improve and enhance customer service at the department level. In the sessions, the facilitators discussed customer service and consumers' shopping experiences. The employees learned that service is an important customer driver. Some employees had difficulty seeing how service relates to the competing health care marketplace. It is exciting to view the learning process and see discovery of knowledge in action. The organization is working toward harvesting the knowledge as a future benchmark and sharing information and resources interdepartmentally.

### Targeted Issues and Measures

Identifying areas that require benchmarking is important. Spending time thinking about the issue that requires resolution is vital. Managers should begin this step by concentrating on analyzing the problem or opportunity. Writing down responses to the questions in Figure 4–1 will reveal the specific issues that must be resolved. It is not the time to attempt to arrive at solutions to the problem or opportunity.

A focused inquiry provides an in-depth review of the situation. It gives the respondent the opportunity to think about possible root causes and to look beyond surface symptoms. When dealing with top management, HR professionals must document their activities and the results. Data must be in quantifiable numbers (cost, time, benefits, quantity, percentages, numbers, dollars, differences, trends, profit/loss).

To use benchmarking successfully, HR professionals need clearly defined measures of competency and performance. However, the paradox is that few clearly defined measures and even fewer standard approaches exist to benchmark against in human resources. The benchmarking process can be time consuming, and information can be difficult to obtain. Many companies rely on outside help to contact competitors to collect the information they need in developing a benchmark.

## Step 2: Research

Begin the research process by identifying and reviewing available resources (see Figure 4–2). A good start would be checking the availability and extent of online databases with local libraries, colleges, and universities. On-line databases provide access to a variety of resources, including magazines, journals, newspapers, books, reference sources, Internet resources, government publications, conference publications, and transcripts of radio and television news programs. The challenge of such research is to focus on a specific issue. For instance, some individuals will focus too closely on details and miss the bigger picture, while others will conduct a search that is too broad in scope.

*Figure 4-1* ———————————————————————————————

## Focused Inquiry

1. Describe the basic problem or opportunity.
2. What are the major factors involved?
3. When did it become a problem or opportunity?
4. Why is it important enough to study?
5. Is there any relevant data available on the problem or opportunity?
6. Where is the problem or opportunity located?
7. Who is involved or affected?
8. Describe the current status.
9. Describe the desired status.
10. Analyze the problem or opportunity for symptoms versus possible causes.
11. List all possible explanations for the problem or opportunity.
12. Which of the above explanations appear the most relevant?
13. Are there any common relationships among the explanations?
14. On the basis of a review of the major causes of the problem or opportunity, is it realistic to reduce, modify, or eliminate one or more of them?
15. Specifically, in what practical ways will the situation improve if the problem or opportunity is solved?
16. How will the organization benefit?
17. Is it likely that top management will commit to and support the effort?
18. What is your personal involvement with the problem?
19. What degree of control do you have over the situation?
20. What first few steps can you identify that need to be taken?
21. Write the specific, targeted issue as a statement or question. Identify where the problem is found, the major factors involved, and who is affected.

*Figure 4-2*

## Sources of Information

| | |
|---|---|
| Review of Baldrige Award Winners | Universities |
| Literature Review (periodical library searches, published books) | Customers, Suppliers, and Stakeholders |
| | Internal and External Experts |
| Participation in Benchmarking Forums | Trade Publications |
| Questions to On-line Message Boards | Research Studies |
| On-line Benchmarking Studies | Surveys |
| Consultants | Focus Groups |
| Internet Sites | Site Visits |
| Benchmarking Reports | Consortiums |
| Networking Sources | Trade Associations |
| Associations | Chambers of Commerce |
| Publications | Award-Winning Companies |

The data collected must be meaningful and useful and must focus on the problem or opportunity statement, including the who, what, where, and why. The research will be easier if the researcher looks for possible solutions rather than efforts supporting the proposed solution. The researcher must realize that hundreds of databases are available, databases are selective in their coverage, and retrieval from them is based on key indexes. In looking for information, the researcher may find it necessary to search several indexes. For example, a search on the topic of employee turnover will retrieve thousands of sources. The researcher should focus on the problem or opportunity statement. A focused statement identifies the key words, descriptors, and subjects—making for better retrieval of relevant citations. Examples of a focused search statement are employee turnover and salaries, employee turnover and morale, and employee turnover and information technology.

The second phase in the research process is to network with colleagues through professional and trade associations, chambers of commerce, and so forth. An Internet search engine will help the researcher find a variety of networking opportunities via web pages for professional and trade associations and for state, federal, and global resources.

The third phase is to consider contacting other organizations. Some organizations are willing to share data and discuss their practices. The researcher starts this phase by developing a contact list and tightly focused questions for each intended contact (see Figure 4–3).

*Figure 4-3*

## Focused Inquiry Questions
## Survey Subject: Tuition Reimbursement
## Caps and Policy Changes

1.  Does the company have a tuition reimbursement dollar cap in place for under graduate- and graduate-level programs and related expenses?
2.  If yes, what is the dollar amount/percentage of coverage for each type of program?
3.  If there is a dollar cap, what factors were considered in setting the amount of the cap?
4.  Is there a payback policy in place?
5.  If yes, are employees required to sign a repayment contract?
6.  Is a length-of-stay requirement part of the repayment contract?
7.  If yes, what is the employment time frame covered by the repayment contract?
8.  Is the company considering any changes to its tuition reimbursement policy in the year ahead?
9.  If yes, what changes are expected?
10. What industry is the company in?
11. What is the approximate number of total employees?

A code of conduct is available on-line at the web site for the International Benchmarking Clearinghouse of the American Productivity and Quality Center. A code of conduct offers advice on how to ethically and effectively engage in best practices studies.

## Step 3: Analysis

In benchmarking, no standard methods or criteria exist to identify and evaluate practices as the best. When reviewing the data collected, the researcher should look for real-world examples of processes, methods, and measures of results, activities, and techniques that culminated in effective performance. The researcher focuses on the purpose and background of the example (without becoming too focused on a particular industry) and tries to differentiate between "good to know" and "need to know" information. The information collected must be compared against the questions posed in Figure 4–1 (specifically the question concerning desired status) and common findings, suggested improvements, and gaps in the data must be sought. Finally, the researcher should continue to ask more questions, such as

- When did the change occur?
- How did the change support the goals of the organization?
- What was the lesson learned?
- What quantitative and qualitative data were collected?
- How were the data collected?
- How were the data measured?
- What were the results?
- Were the measurements calculated differently from the data collected?
- What elements fit into the organization's cultural environment?
- What changes will the organization need to make to produce improvement?

Measurement comparisons are to be approached warily; they may lead to comparing "apples" with "oranges." Practices that are effective in one organization will not necessarily work in another, but ideas can be modified and adapted.

At this point, the development of recommendations and action plan suggestions are in order. The action plans should include a time line and identify who will be accountable for what.

## Step 4: Implementation

Implementing change to ensure continuous improvement is necessary. To add value to the organization, HR must be willing to take action. This value-added mentality is evident throughout each of the four steps of the benchmarking process. Step 1, planning, looked at what is and what is not working by documenting, measuring, and analyzing HR processes. Step 2, research, provided the opportunity to identify benchmarking sources. Step 3 involved analysis of real-world examples of processes, methods, and measures of results, activities, and techniques that culminated in effective performance. Benchmarking is key to developing clearly defined measures of competency and performance in HR. Numbers lend credibility to the HR function, and data support comparisons and provide a way to gauge progress. Finally, step 4 shows that communication and action must follow the benchmarking effort. Implementation tips and strategies are as follows:

- Communicate findings to top management.
- Present findings as bullet points.
- Display results of data in graphic form (e.g., bar graphs, pie charts).
- Identify opportunities for improvement.
- Gain commitment and support from top management.
- Establish goals.
- Develop measurable objectives, or desired outcomes (e.g., within 3 months of the implementation, the total number of serious accidents will decrease by 20% over a comparable period a year earlier).
- Achieve buy-in by involving key people in the implementation efforts.
- Implement specific changes.
- Communicate.
- Monitor progress.
- To remain current, redefine benchmarks and review processes every 2 to 3 years.

## References and Suggested Readings

American Productivity and Quality Center (APQC). [On-line]. Available: <http://www.apqc.org/>.

The Benchmarking Exchange. [On-line]. Available: <http://www.benchnet.com>.

Fitz-enz, J. (1995). *How to measure human resource management.* New York: McGraw-Hill.

Gray, D. A. (1997). *360° analysis of how HR adds value to an organization.* SHRM/CCH Survey.

Grossman, R. J. (2000, January). Measuring up. *HRMagazine, 45,* 29–35.

Hennessey, H.W. (1997) Measuring added value and effectiveness. In M. Singer & M. Fleming (Eds.), *Effective human resources measurement techniques: A handbook for practitioners.* Alexandria, VA: Society for Human Resource Management.

Hennessey, H. W. (1998). *Simple descriptive statistics for HR manager* (SHRM Management Practices White Paper). Alexandria, VA: Society for Human Resource Management.

Phillips, J. J. (1996). *Accountability in human resource management.* Houston, TX: Gulf Publishing.

Rothwell, W. J., Prescott, R. K., & Taylor, M. W. (1998). *Strategic Human Resource Leader.* Palo Alto, CA: Davies-Black Publishing.

Swist, J. (1997). Benchmarking in human resources. (SHRM Management Practices White Paper). Alexandria, VA: Society for Human Resource Management.

## Chapter 5

# Measuring, Analyzing, and Communicating Employee Turnover

*Rose Howse*

Turnover is costly to organizations. Additional recruitment, training and re-training, and performance losses attributable to unwanted turnover cost the organization in time and money and affect employee morale. Analyzing turnover can help reduce or prevent losses through organizational improvements. (See chapter 6 for additional discussion of costs of turnover.)

The calculation of turnover is a simple mathematical problem. The analysis of turnover is a powerful tool the human resource (HR) profession uses to interpret movement of employees into, within, and out of organizations. Turnover is often the first measurement that organization leadership requests when it is contemplating proposals for scarce resources, implementing new programs, or looking at whether change efforts have been successful. Knowing turnover rates is a necessity in any organization, but rates alone may lack significance. Analysis and interpretation of turnover are a valued contribution the HR department can make to the organization.

Although turnover analysis contributes to understanding the organization, it is rare that the HR practitioners can show a direct cause and effect relationship between turnover and specific organizational variables. However, HR professionals can usually illustrate a relationship between organizational changes and employee reactions such as turnover. Results of turnover analysis can help focus the strategic HR function on areas of concern, targets for change efforts, or areas of success in the organization. Turnover is one widely accepted indicator of how the business is doing from an employment perspective.

## Relevance of Turnover

Turnover is the permanent separation of employees from a position, a department, or an organization. Because there are numerous origins of turnover, it may be related to several aspects of the organization and its environment. Turnover originates from promotion or demotion, transfer, resignation, termination, or retirement of employees. Selection systems, compensation, benefits, performance management, managerial talent, training effectiveness, organizational policies, and the organization's external environment influence and are influenced by employee turnover. Increasing trends in turnover may be symptomatic of isolated or systemic issues that require change or intervention within the organization. Conversely, decreasing trends in organizational turnover may indicate changes in the labor market or other societal factors, or they may indicate the success of a specific new program. Within an organization, HR practitioners may use decreasing trends in turnover to indicate a relationship between HR programs and organizational success. Turnover analysis helps illustrate this relationship between internal or external factors and organizational success.

For example, if new technology were recently added to a job and turnover began to increase among employees in that job, several factors may be contributing to the increase in turnover. Turnover analysis prompts the questions Who is leaving? Is the turnover voluntary or involuntary? and What is this new skill worth in the labor market?

First, if the employees who are leaving are predominantly employees new to the job, the turnover could indicate an out-of-date selection system that fails to address the new job skill requirements. Increasing turnover in the job among long-term employees may indicate ineffectiveness or lack of training in the new technology. Second, if the turnover is voluntary (such as in a transfer or resignation), employees may self-select out of the job or the organization because they do not have the skills needed to perform the work. If the turnover is involuntary, the manager of the work may be releasing employees from the organization because they are unable to adequately perform the work. Third, the market for employees who are familiar with the new technology may dictate a higher wage for their work than what the organization pays.

### Looking for Causes Behind the Trends
In analyzing turnover, HR practitioners need to contemplate what influences could be contributing to trends in turnover. There may be a new manager in a department that is experiencing increased turnover. The manager may not have the training or managerial skills needed or may have a managerial style that contradicts organizational culture expectations. The manager may enforce policies more strictly, resulting in an increase in terminations, or may be less attentive to

development, resulting in an increase in resignations. The organization may have made changes that affect employees' personal lives, such as a change in hours of operation. The change may contribute to an increase in turnover as employees seek positions with more desirable hours. Implementation of a stricter attendance policy may influence both voluntary and involuntary employee turnover.

The organization may also have implemented changes that contribute to a decrease in turnover. A recent increase in wages means the organization is more competitive in the labor market. Implementation of family-friendly programs may contribute to a better work and family balance, thus reducing turnover. It is important for HR practitioners to understand the concept of turnover, measure it, analyze it, and present its relationship to organizational outcomes that directly affect organizational success.

### "Good" Turnover Versus "Bad" Turnover

Organizations do not want zero turnover. Not all turnover is "bad" for organizational outcomes. Turnover initiated by the company is generally thought of as "good" or acceptable turnover; in other words, it is the result of upholding policy and performance expectations. For example, the turnover that results from terminating an employee for violation of harassment policies is good for the organization. Allowing harassment or similar situations to continue could have disastrous legal implications for the company, be detrimental to the morale of other employees, and actually contribute to a number of other unwanted organizational outcomes.

"Bad" or unacceptable turnover generally exists when good employees leave voluntarily. The organization is not meeting the desired employment outcomes for these employees. Investments in the exiting employee (i.e., hiring, training, and salary costs) and performance losses (e.g., "downtime," increased hours for other employees) occur when high-performing, newly trained, or key employees leave the organization. Although this chapter focuses on preventable voluntary turnover, involuntary turnover can also reveal important trends that require intervention.

## Importance of Defining Terms

HR and organizations use turnover measurement and its changes over time to analyze aspects of employment. Therefore, it is important to standardize a definition within the organization that provides the information needed. When deciding how to define the calculation of turnover, HR practitioners must think broadly about what the organization needs or wants to know about turnover.

It may be very important to the organization to compare internal turnover rates to a published industry standard. Comparison to a standard measurement requires that internal turnover be calculated exactly the same as the standard. For example, if the published standard being used as a baseline measurement does not include part-time employees, that group cannot be included in the organization measurement or the comparison will be misleading. However, the organization may have a large number of part-time employees and find it important to include them in the turnover calculation. If so, comparison to the standard may be less meaningful than comparison to other organizations or units that also include part-time employees in the calculation. Depending on what the organization is trying to determine from turnover analysis, needs may dictate that HR practitioners deviate from the standard to provide meaningful information.

The Bureau of National Affairs (BNA) provides a definition of turnover, and its calculation has become the standard by which the HR profession *generally* measures turnover. National quarterly data from the BNA provide a standard measurement to compare turnover among organizations and within industries. To use the BNA data to compare organizations, turnover must be measured by using the exact method employed by the BNA. The BNA defines "turnover" as all permanent separations of employees, whether voluntary or involuntary. The definition seems clear-cut. However, unless we know the meaning of the terms used in the definition, we could make misleading comparisons of the organization to this published standard.

"Separations" is defined as permanent disassociations from the group, such as termination, resignation, and retirement. It does not include temporary separations such as employees placed on temporary or indefinite layoff or employees who are on temporary leaves of absence. "Employees" is defined as "regular" employees and does not include temporary help, part-time employees, or interns. (BNA).

The calculation for turnover is the number of separations from the group being analyzed divided by the average number of employees in the group. For an organization, the calculation is

$$\frac{\text{Number of permanent separations for the month}}{\text{Average number of employees on payroll for the month}} \times 100 = \text{Turnover percentage rate}$$

The following scenario illustrates the calculation. An organization had an average of 100 employees last month. Nine employees resigned for such reasons as "better opportunity," "more money," and "closer to home." One employee retired. Five employees were terminated because of poor performance, on-the-job altercation, third written warning for absences, and so forth. Five more employees were terminated for failing to report to work for 3 days without calling in. One employee left for a 30-day personal leave of absence. Hence, 20 permanent separations occurred last month. The employee on leave of absence is not included because that person is expected to return after 30 days.

According to the BNA turnover formula, the number of permanent separations for the month (20) is divided by the average employers for the month (100). Thus, the turnover rate for last month is 20%.

Although the BNA measurement is a widely accepted standard that provides a means of comparison among organizations and industries, HR practitioners may need to further refine the definition to analyze the data and provide information needed by the organization. Following is an example of how the definition of terms for the calculation of turnover affects the outcome of the measurement.

Is it best to measure voluntary versus involuntary turnover or preventable versus nonpreventable turnover in a particular organization? Within that organization, what types of separations are voluntary? Resignations and retirements are generally voluntary; if an organization really wants to measure preventable turnover, however, including retirements in the calculation will overstate the resulting rate. Conversely, excluding employees who do not come to work and do not call in to explain their absence (commonly called "3-day no-call, no shows") may understate preventable turnover. In many organizations, terminations of employees who fail to follow an attendance policy may be considered involuntary turnover. However, if the organization decides that those employees have resigned without notice, such terminations may be considered as voluntary or preventable turnover. It is important to decide exactly what the organization needs to measure. Doing so helps define what does or does not go into the calculation and what the measurement is "telling" the organization.

In the example described above, if only the nine official resignations and the one retirement are included in the calculation, the rate would be

$$\frac{10 \text{ voluntary permanent separations}}{100 \text{ employees (average)}} = .10 \times 100 = 10\%$$

The organization might be comfortable with 10% voluntary turnover. But there were five employees who were terminated because they stopped coming to work. If those employees are considered voluntary separations (resigned without notice) for turnover calculation purposes, the voluntary rate would be

$$\frac{15 \text{ voluntary permanent separations}}{100 \text{ employees (average)}} = .15 \times 100 = 15\%$$

The organization may or may not be comfortable with 15% voluntary turnover. However, if the no-call, no-shows had not been included in the calculation, voluntary turnover in the organization would be understated. The organization may really want to know how much preventable turnover there was. If the organization considers the no-call, no-shows voluntary resignations and considers all nonretirement resignations preventable, only the 9 resignations and the 5 no-call, no-shows would have been included. In this case, the result is a more accurate preventable turnover percentage rate of 14%.

Those types of issues need to be decided when defining how and why the organization will measure turnover. Defining exactly what is to be measured and deciding what is or is not to be included in the calculation are important not only in the calculation itself, but also in the analysis and presentation of the results. People interpret turnover measurement in different ways. If different people are providing measurements from different units to contribute to an overall organizational measure, each person needs to fully understand what to include in the calculation. Users of the data also need to fully understand what is included in order to draw accurate conclusions from the data.

## Sample Analysis
### Turnover Rates
Once an organization decides exactly what is needed in the measurement of turnover, HR practitioners can dig even deeper into its analysis. Turnover rates compare organizations or groups within organizations. HR can track these rates over time to determine cyclical trends in turnover or if certain events contribute to sudden changes in the rate. The following data bring a number of questions to mind:

| | |
|---|---|
| June | 8% |
| July | 6% |
| August | 12% |
| September | 8% |
| October | 7% |

November  5%

December  2%

What looks like a significant change in the turnover rate occurred in August and December. What could be causing the changes? Is the organization unknowingly hiring students who had intentions of working only for the summer? Possibly, a new policy or program was implemented in July that affected turnover for August. A decrease in turnover may be a normal phenomenon as employees "stick it out" for holiday spending needs or to obtain the organization's holiday bonus.

Determining what organizational units or employee groups are most vulnerable to high turnover can help concentrate intervention efforts. Conversely, knowing which groups are experiencing less turnover may help determine whether there are some intraorganizational best practices that could be expanded to other areas. Turnover analysis, in conjunction with exit interviews (which ask "Why are you leaving?") and retention interviews (which ask "Why are you staying?"), can help HR determine not only "what's wrong" but also "what's working" within the organization.

The following hypothetical example compares turnover rates within departments to determine whether specific employee groups are more susceptible to preventable turnover. HR practitioners need to look at the average number of employees in the month for each department and the number of preventable voluntary separations within each group. The data appear in Table 5–1.

*Table 5-1*

## Comparative Turnover Rates

| Department | Average Employees | Preventable Separations | Rate (%) |
|---|---|---|---|
| Human Resources | 10 | 1 | 10.0 |
| Information Systems | 50 | 11 | 22.0 |
| Finance | 24 | 2 | 8.3 |
| Maintenance | 50 | 0 | 0.0 |
| Overall Total | 134 | 14 | 10.4 |

The highest rate is in the Information Systems (IS) department. This information helps focus the analysis on attempting to find out why IS professionals are leaving. Less than competitive salary rates for this "hot skills" area, being asked to work long hours on specific projects, or the lack of development opportunities to keep IS professionals current in their profession may all be reasons contributing to turnover in that department. The maintenance department shows no preventable turnover; its manager may be offering special incentives, using a rotating or flex schedule, paying more competitively, or spending extra time sharing new skills with employees.

## Analysis of Other Types of Turnover

Proportions of types of turnover and characteristics of separated employees can also be analyzed in order to provide information as to who is leaving the organization and what might prevent turnover.

Knowing the overall turnover rate helps compare organizations. Knowing the proportion of voluntary to involuntary turnover may also be helpful. An overall rate of 20%, compared to an industry average of 25%, may be acceptable to an organization. But some of that turnover may be preventable. Additional analysis may help HR practitioners determine whether some of the turnover could have been avoided. Of the 20 employees who permanently separated, maybe only 6 employees left because of involuntary termination and the other 14 employees voluntarily resigned. In such a case, the total separations constitute the divisor and the preventable separations the numerator:

$$\frac{14 \text{ preventable separations}}{20 \text{ total separations}} = .7 \times 100 = 70\%$$

According to the calculation, 70% of the turnover might have been prevented! If it had been prevented, the overall rate would have been only 6% (6 employees of the 100 average employees for the month left the organization). Rather than being comfortable with having a turnover below the industry average, the organization might have been considered an "employer of choice."

To find out when employees tend to leave an organization, HR practitioners would again look at only the group of employees who have left the organization. Pertinent data list the employees and their length of service.

| | |
|---|---|
| Employee A | 19.0 months |
| Employee B | 20.0 months |
| Employee C | 60.0 months |
| Employee D | 19.0 months |

| | | |
|---|---|---|
| Employee E | 21.0 months | |
| Employee F | 20.0 months | |
| Employee G | 1.0 month | |
| Employee H | 1.5 months | |
| Employee I | 0.5 month | |
| Employee J | 1.0 month | |

According to these data, the average length of service of the employees who have left the organization can be calculated at about 16 months. That figure may or may not be helpful information for the organization. HR practitioners may wish to look for patterns within the length of service. For example, five of the employees (50%) had between 19 and 21 months of service, four employees (40%) had 1.5 months or less, and one had 5 years of service. A pattern emerges when analyzing data in this manner. Employees seem to be experiencing "decision" points at around 30 days, 18 months, and 5 years of service. Further analysis may determine what happens to employees at those points in their service. HR may create and implement some programs targeted to those points or add other data points to further refine the analysis. For example, looking at the departments that the employees worked in may provide additional valuable information.

| | | |
|---|---|---|
| Employee A | 19.0 months | IS |
| Employee B | 20.0 months | IS |
| Employee C | 60.0 months | HR |
| Employee D | 19.0 months | IS |
| Employee E | 21.0 months | IS |
| Employee F | 20.0 months | IS |
| Employee G | 1.0 month | PR |
| Employee H | 1.5 months | PR |
| Employee I | 0.5 month | PR |
| Employee J | 1.0 month | PR |

Analyzing the turnover data can provide some valuable insights for HR practitioners. They can determine not only the length of service of those employees who left, but also what proportion of employees were from what departments. Five of the 10 separations (50%) are from the IS department, and the IS employees who are leaving are doing so soon after the 18-month mark. The organization may have a training or incentive program in the IS department that is 18 months in length. If so, the HR department may suggest implementation of further retention bonuses, a pay-back clause in a training agreement, or improvement in selection for the training program. Conversely, in the production (PR) department, where 40% of the turnover occurred, the length of service of those employees who have left the organization is much shorter. Perhaps there is a need in that department for a realistic job preview or for improved orientation and training programs. Armed with such information, HR practitioners may decide to create or strengthen retention programs and re-recruitment efforts aimed at the employees who are about to reach length-of-service milestones. Continued analysis of the data after implementation of improvements may provide additional data showing the effectiveness of the turnover intervention.

Other characteristics that HR practitioners may wish to analyze include specific professions (e.g., programmers, nurses), sex, age group, ethnicity, or shift. In the IS separations, if four of the five employees who left were programmers, we can say that 40% of the total turnover for the month consisted of programmers:

$$\frac{4 \text{ programmers}}{10 \text{ total separations}} = .4 \times 100 = 40\%$$

And, we can say that 80% of the turnover in the IS department consisted of programmers:

$$\frac{4 \text{ programmers}}{5 \text{ IS separations}} = .8 \times 100 = 80\%$$

HR practitioners should be open to unexpected results. In a company in which the author analyzed turnover, we were surprised to find, contrary to assumptions, that night shifts did not have higher turnover rates than day shifts. This finding helped the organization change its assumptions and caused it to look deeper into the data to find out what was different about the night shifts.

## Presentation of Data

Today's presentation, spreadsheet, and graphing software make it easy to create highly professional presentations of turnover data. As HR practitioners are increasingly called to the table as a strategic partner, it is more important for all HR practitioners to become comfortable with software tools. Most introductory courses in spreadsheet software will include the basics of graphing. Once the HR practitioner is comfortable with navigating the software, experimenting with the different options is an extremely valuable learning activity that can be applied in HR work immediately.

Determining what purpose turnover analysis is used for within the organization will help dictate how the information is best presented to users of the data. If the organization measures the effect of managerial performance on turnover, analyzing by manager or department is important and may be reported with bar or column graphs as well as time-series analysis. If the company is concerned with the number of employees it loses from its workforce because of Equal Opportunity Employment or Affirmative Action concerns, or if a certain benefit such as day care will help retain workers, the company may want to use pie charts to analyze and report by employee demographic characteristics. Although it is always important to know the needs and preferences of the audience (e.g., some managers prefer tabled data versus charts, or vice versa), some simple guidelines can help the HR practitioner focus the audience on the desired objectives of the presentation.

## Written Reports

Generally, it is helpful to give a snapshot of "how things are," show changes from the last report, and discuss possible contributing factors and solutions. A written report should begin with a summary page that includes definitions of terms and shows comparison data. Busy executives appreciate concise information and often prefer to see basic information at a glance. A table format with comparison and summary data can provide very good information in a small amount of space and allow the user to draw overview conclusions such as "turnover is going down." This type of overview invites users to "dig in" to the details at their convenience (see Table 5–2).

*Table 5-2*

| Measure | This Period | Last Period | % Change |
|---|---|---|---|
| Overall Rate | 12% | 14% | +16.7% |
| Voluntary Rate | 7% | 5% | -28.6% |
| Involuntary Rate | 5% | 9% | +80% |

In this example in Table 5–2 definitions of "overall," "voluntary," and "involuntary" would appear on the summary page to accompany the table.

Later pages of the report include text and discussion regarding observations of trends, recent changes in the organization that may or may not have influenced the results, and any plans that may be under development for addressing the issues. A table of contents or an index of graphs included in the report allows the user to pinpoint where particular information can be found in the report. Graphic presentations can be included within the body of the report or as appendices.

## Charts

Generally, for showing trends over time, a line graph is effective. A time line can represent monthly, quarterly, or annual periods. It may be helpful to report time-based measurements in ways similar to other departments within the organization. For example, quarterly reporting might be the norm in an organization. From the example of monthly rates in Table 5–2, the HR practitioner might graph a time line such as the chart in Figure 5–1.

*Figure 5-1*

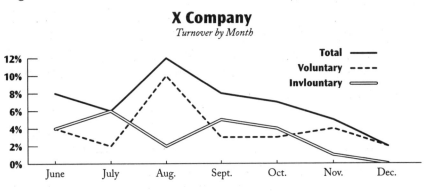

For comparisons of turnover among groups, a standard column chart is helpful. See Figure 5–2.

For proportions or characteristics of subgroups (e.g., preventable separations only), a pie chart or a stacked column graph can be helpful. For example, using a pie chart to show reasons given by the employees who have voluntarily left the organization helps the audience see not only the "big picture," but also the separate components. See Figures 5–3, 5–4, and 5–5.

For comparing different entities in conjunction with other slices of the data (e.g., reasons for separation by department), a stacked column graph is effective. Following is a comparison of different entities (departments in this case) and the distribution of turnover reasons for separation for each. (See Figure 5–6.) This type of graph helps pinpoint areas of concern. In one business unit the issues may be compensation related, but in another issues may be based on lack of training.

*Figure 5-2*

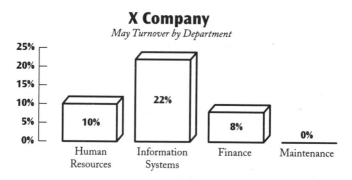

**X Company**
*May Turnover by Department*

*Figure 5-3*

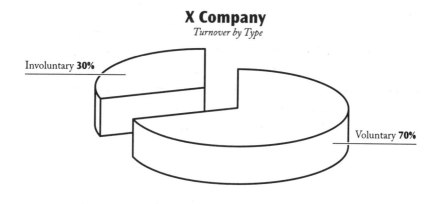

**X Company**
*Turnover by Type*

### Tips for Effective Presentation

Titles for graphs are extremely important. The time period and group that the chart or graph describes should always be included. For example, a chart showing voluntary turnover for a specific department for a specific month should have a title as descriptive as "Voluntary HR Department Turnover in September 1999." Or if the chart shows turnover by the same department over several months, it may have a title of "1999 Voluntary HR Department Turnover by Month."

Figure 5-4

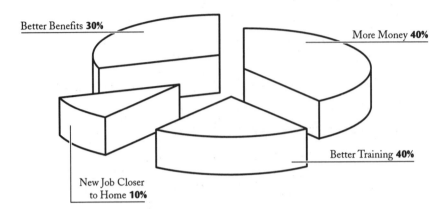

**X Company**
*Voluntary Turnover by Reason*

Better Benefits **30%**

More Money **40%**

Better Training **40%**

New Job Closer
to Home **10%**

Figure 5-5

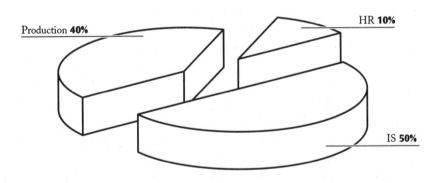

**X Company**
*Preventable Turnover by Department*

Production **40%**

HR **10%**

IS **50%**

Having definitions of terms in the chart is also very helpful to the user. For example, a chart of "voluntary turnover" should include the organization's definition of the term, such as, "Voluntary turnover is defined as the number of permanent employee–initiated separations but does not include temporary or part-time employees, interns, retirements or temporary absences." The text box feature of most spreadsheet software can be used to add the definition directly to the chart, or the definition can be added to the margin footer.

*Figure 5-6*

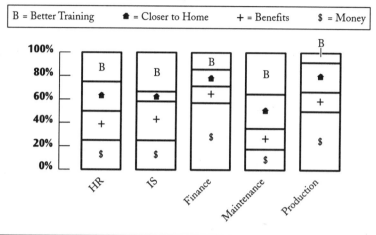

# X Company
*Voluntary Turnover by Department and Reason*

B = Better Training    ♠ = Closer to Home    + = Benefits    $ = Money

Copy and paste functions can be used to bring spreadsheet charts into the text area of the report document. If the report is placed on an intranet or in a shared folder of the organization's computer network, hyperlinks can easily be created in the table of contents or the chart index to allow the user to "jump" to the charts within the report. Most software provides information on how to create hyperlinks within and between documents. Generally, a bookmark is created where the chart is located (where the user will jump to). A hyperlink is created in the index (where the user will jump from). The two are linked by "telling" the hyperlink the name of the bookmark that the user will get to when clicking on the underlined blue hyperlink.

Spreadsheet, graphing, and presentation software also allows the HR practitioner to be creative in the use of subliminal clues that influence the audience. For example, in black and white graphs, shading that shows increasing levels of turnover can create a sense of urgency. Use of color in graphs can have even more dramatic effects. Using green to illustrate voluntary turnover (employees are going) and yellow to illustrate involuntary turnover (employees are exercising caution) can underscore differences in acceptable versus unacceptable types of turnover. For daring software adventurers, increasing monthly turnover can be illustrated as low turnover in the first column. Over time, as turnover increases and the column grows, they can try to gradually change the color from blue (complacency?) to yellow (caution) to red (stop!) by using gradient, textured, or patterned "fill effect" on each column. Dramatic color use can influence your audience to take action.

### Consistency in Reporting

Periodic reporting of turnover is highly recommended. The audience would find it helpful to have the presentation appear in a standard format each period. Such standardization helps the audience concentrate on the trends rather than on figuring out the legend keys. For example, in a line graph that compares overall, voluntary, and involuntary time lines, the preparer of the graphics should use the same color for each line each time the data are reported. The overall time line could always appears in red, the voluntary in green, and the involuntary in yellow. For black and white presentations, solid, dotted, and dashed lines can be used as shown in the time line in Figure 5–1.

### "Talking the Talk"

In organizational terms, the HR department's "business" is to provide a high-quality product (i.e., the organization) to the customer (i.e., the labor market). In effect, HR professionals are marketing the organization to labor market consumers through such components as compensation, benefits, culture, working conditions, employment stability, and growth opportunities. Organizations have become the product; job seekers and employees have become the customers. HR professionals can help their organization understand turnover by borrowing some business measurements to describe turnover. Other measurements used in the organization that can be converted to percentages can be compared to turnover percentages to allow managers in all sectors to speak the same language.

In the manufacturing sector, for example, quality control departments track goods returned for quality problems (i.e., products rejected by the customer) in terms of external parts per million, or external ppms. Supervisors, managers, and business leaders in manufacturing are familiar with the term. They generally understand the issues that contribute to an increase in ppm, and they understand some things they can do to reduce ppm. Reporting turnover in terms of ppm can be a valuable eye-opener for manufacturing management. Voluntary turnover of 20% corresponds to a rejection rate of 200,000 ppm! In other words, out of the 1 million employees hired by the organization, 200,000 of these labor market consumers would be dissatisfied enough with the "product" to "return" it by leaving the organization. Such a high ppm rate in product quality usually results in swift and extreme actions to determine the root cause and to correct the problem.

Another example of a common business measurement that can help HR practitioners to communicate turnover results is a customer satisfaction index. Again, this measure, based on a scale of 1 to 10 or 1 to 100, allows easy conversion of a percentage-based measure such as turnover. For example, if turnover is measured among new hires in a 1-year period and found to be 25%, the HR practitioner can state an extrapolated employee retention index of 75 (on a scale of 100) among this group. Increasing this index (i.e., reducing turnover) can become a measurable goal that is easily understood by the leaders in the organization.

HR practitioners should try to find common language in the organization that can be translated to present turnover information. Utilization rates, uptime, downtime, many financial measures, or anything that is expressed as a proportion or a percentage can be used to create common discussion around turnover in the organization.

## Conclusion

Turnover analysis is a valuable contribution that HR practitioners can make to their organization. This tool allows HR practitioners to determine issues that affect the success of the organization. Turnover directly affects costs in the organization, including the costs related to recruitment, training, and performance. BNA defines "turnover" as all permanent separations of employees, whether voluntary or involuntary. Although this measurement allows comparison against a standard benchmark, HR practitioners may need to modify internal definitions to provide the best possible information for the organization's purposes. Communicating turnover results includes finding creative ways to help others in the organization understand and act to prevent unwanted turnover. Detailed text reports, charts and graphs, and a common language used within the organization contribute to valuable discussion of turnover and ways to resolve issues that contribute to turnover and thereby affect success within the organization.

## References and Suggested Readings

Bloch, F. (1997). *Statistics for non-statisticians.* Washington, DC: Equal Employment Advisory Council.

Bureau of National Affairs. *BNA quarterly report on employee turnover.* Washington, DC: Author.

Fitz-enz, J. (1995). *How to measure human resources management.* New York: McGraw-Hill.

Mercer, W. (1989). *Turning your human resources department into a profit center.* New York: American Management Association.

Swanson, R., & Holton III, E. (1997). *Human resource development research handbook: Linking research and practice.* San Francisco: Berrett-Kohler.

Williams, R. W. (1999). Head off turnover at the selection pass. *Employment Management Today 4*(4), 22–26.

# Chapter 6

# Measuring Recruitment

*Jennifer B. Wilson*

**M**easuring your organization's recruitment efforts and the results from those efforts can provide answers to the following important questions: How are we doing? Can we do better? Where should we focus our efforts to improve?

Recruitment provides a pool of potentially qualified candidates from which the organization can select employees who not only meet the needs of the organization but also fulfill their own requirements. Successful recruitment leads to a higher quality of work life for employees and to higher organizational productivity. Recruitment is done within a changing and often costly legal environment, and human resource (HR) professionals must ensure that procedures are in compliance with the law and are well documented to avoid needless and costly legal battles. Measurement is critical in ensuring that HR professionals are effectively and efficiently meeting each of the purposes of recruitment and in guiding changes if the data indicating that changes are necessary.

Because finding and hiring the best employees are critical to an organization's success, one would think that systematic, formal measurement would be the standard practice for HR professionals. The 14th annual research study conducted by the Society for Human Resource Management (SHRM) and the Commerce Clearing House (CCH) and presented at the 1999 SHRM conference revealed some pertinent information on HR recruitment practices and beliefs in U.S. organizations (Wilson, 1999). The study found that less than half (44%) of the respondents conduct any formal evaluation of the effect of their recruitment effort, despite the costs involved in the critical HR function of recruiting new employees.

Cost-efficient recruitment affects an organization's profit as well as its strategic plans. More than ever, selecting employees who meet the needs of the organization is a major factor distinguishing successful organizations from unsuccessful organizations. Measurement that establishes a baseline provides data on the real value of new methods of recruitment, development, and retention. By carefully identifying current recruitment sources, new sources can be identified and their cost-benefit ratio can be measured. By analyzing each step or method in recruitment, the most cost-efficient and effective recruitment can be conducted by an organization and modified as changes occur in the work environment.

## What to Measure

The first question you need to ask is what to measure. The answer depends on what you want to learn. You must determine what purpose the data analysis serves for your recruiters, line and middle managers, division chairs, CEO, and board of directors. Your internal customers may not have thought through what they need. It will be up to you to advise them in order to determine their needs and to decide how to best serve those needs. For example, managers who experience high turnover rates may want you to deliver qualified candidates in large numbers. During times of full employment, this request may not be possible to meet. The real need is for qualified employees who will stay with the organization for longer periods of time. Your real service may be in determining the characteristics of those employees whose work is satisfactory or outstanding and who have a long tenure with the company, and then determining how to attract and identify similar job applicants. Without ongoing communication, it may appear to the managers that you are ignoring their immediate needs. Honest, problem-solving communication with your managers and other customers will be essential in determining their long-term needs and how you can meet those needs.

You may find it useful to consider various criteria for assessing your recruitment processes. One model is presented by Schuler (1992), who lists types of criteria for assessing recruitment by the stage of the applicant's or new hire's entry into the organization. At the preentry or advertising stage, Schuler suggests using total number of applicants, number of minority and female applicants, cost per applicant, time to locate applicants, and time to process applicants. At the stage of employment offers and hiring, he suggests measuring offers extended by source, total number of qualified applicants, number of qualified female and minority applicants, applicants with disabilities, and costs of acceptance versus rejection of applicants. At the time of new employees' entry into the organization, Schuler suggests using initial expectations of newcomers, choice of the organization by qualified applicants, cost and time of training new employees, and salary levels. Finally, at postentry, when the employee has been with the organization for a given period of time, he suggests measuring attitudes toward job, pay, benefits, supervision, and co-workers; organizational commitment; job performance; tenure of hires; absenteeism; and referrals. Your objective is not to measure and analyze every possible variable but to select and measure those variables in your organization that will provide the information needed for you to be successful in finding, recruiting and retaining those employees who will make your organization successful.

## Criteria for Assessing Recruitment

### Preentry or advertising stage
- Total number of applicants
- Number of minority and female applicants
- Cost per applicant
- Time to locate applicants
- Time to process applicants

### Employment offers and hiring stage
- Offers extended by source
- Total number of qualified applicants
- Number of qualified female and minority applicants and applicants with disabilities
- Costs of acceptance versus rejection of applicants

### Postentry stage
- Attitudes toward job, pay, benefits, supervision, and co-workers
- Organizational commitment
- Job performance
- Tenure of hires
- Absenteeism
- Referrals

## How to Measure Recruitment

For our purposes, we will separate measurement into three categories (cost, time, tests) and provide formulas and examples for each category. You may find a combination or hybrid of these measurements to be most useful, or you may use these models to create your own measurement system. These formulas and examples for measuring recruitment are not exhaustive; they are intended to get you started. The measurement system you establish will be valuable only if it meets the unique needs of your organization and if the data are turned into information that decision makers can use to make informed decisions. The measurements and their reporting and use will need to fit into the culture of your particular organization. Periodically, you will want to determine if your measurement system continues to meet your organization's needs. Some trial or pilot measures might be useful to explore questions that arise with the evolution of your organization and the labor market. For example, the formula to determine cost per hire includes the cost of employee referrals. However, you may have discovered that using employee referrals is counterproductive to meeting the affirmative action goals of your organization if your employees are not diverse. Employees tend to refer friends and relatives, usually of the same race and age categories. The formula also includes the costs of employing a recruiter. However, your organization may outsource this function. In such cases, the formula would be adjusted to exclude these two factors that are not used in the organization.

## Measuring Cost-Effectiveness

Perhaps the best place to start is with a measure of what it costs to find and hire each person, which is often termed "cost per hire" (CPH). CPH was defined in 1986 by the SHRM/Saratoga Institute Human Resource Effectiveness Report according to the following formula (Fitz-enz, 1995):

$$CPH = \frac{Ad + AF + ER + T + Relo + RC}{H} + 10\%$$

where Ad is advertising costs paid to generate applicants

AF denotes fees paid to agencies to generate applicants

ER is any hire or referral bonuses paid out

T is the travel, lodging, and food costs for staff and candidates

Relo is the relocation costs incurred by the organization

RC is recruiters' salary (broken down to an hourly rate), benefits, and overhead (e.g., space, equipment) multiplied by the number of hours spent per job

H is the number of people hired

10% covers all other expenses incurred (plus or minus 1.5%)

An example of how this formula might look with data from your organization follows:

$$CPH = \frac{\$5{,}000 + \$1{,}000 + \$500 + \$200 + \$0 + \$200}{H} + 10\% = \$230 + \$23 = \$253$$

Although the RC variable in this formula may seem complex and daunting, standard labor costing can reduce it to a manageable and understandable figure. You can determine a standard rate for each level of recruiter who is involved and then determine the average number of hours that that level of recruiter works on each specific class of hires. This figure can then be substituted in the formula. The 10% in the formula covers all other costs, and was found to be accurate within 1.5% in an 8-year study (Fitz-enz, 1995). Once you have determined the cost per hire, you can begin separating cost per hire by the types of expenses. You will discover, in great detail, where you are effective and where you can improve. Fitz-enz provides a model, formulas, and examples of how to conduct your analyses. You can determine the cost of hiring through various sources by using the following formula (Fitz-enz, 1995):

$$SCPH = \frac{AC + AF + RB + NC}{H}$$

where SCPH is the source cost per hire
      AC is advertising costs as total monthly expenditures
      AF is agency fees total for the month
      RB is referral bonuses total paid
      NC is no-cost hires, walk-ins, nonprofit agencies, and so forth
      H is the total number of hires

For example, you may want to determine which sources are most effective in delivering hourly workers for your organization. By comparing this information with the same information for salaried workers, you may find that you can realize cost savings by using similar recruitment sources or that you can make your resources go farther by using distinctly different sources. You could include only exempt hires, nonexempt hires, hourly workers, or other specific job groups in your formulas to answer other questions that you may have about the relative cost of recruitment sources for specific types of hires. This simplified example illustrates how you begin to develop and use measurements to gather and analyze data to direct your hiring efforts. In addition to these analyses, you can divide each recruitment source by the number of hires to show the comparative costs of each hire, as illustrated by the formula and example that follow:

$$SCPH = \frac{AC}{H} + \frac{AF}{H} + \frac{RB}{H} + \frac{NC}{H}$$

$$SCPH = \frac{\$3,000 + \$3,000 + \$2,000 + \$0}{20} = \$400$$

With your average SCPH calculated (in the example it is $400), you can compare the figure to the effect of a special event or new source by listing all expenses incurred (direct and indirect) and dividing by the number of hires in the special event to obtain an absolute return on investment (ROI). If your organization spent $5,000 on a career fair (for materials, employee salaries/benefits, travel, etc.) and hired 40 employees as a result, your cost per hire for the special event would be $125 ($5,000/40), which would be less costly than your standard cost per hire of $400. No HR department can claim to operate efficiently if it does not know how much it is spending to hire people (Fitz-enz, 1995).

An efficient method of analyzing the above data is to compare total costs by the type of hire and to compare each type of cost by the type of hire. If the only comparisons are between the broad categories of exempt and nonexempt positions (as defined in the Fair Labor Standards Act), the results will be predictable. You would expect the total costs to hire executives to be higher than the total costs to hire custodians. However, comparisons between different categories of nonexempt positions or between positions within different divisions of the organization will provide much more useful information.

For example, if you find it more expensive to hire accountants than salespersons, your next steps are to find out why and to determine ways to reduce the cost of hiring accountants. By comparing each type of cost (e.g., advertising, agency fees, referral bonuses, travel, relocation) to each type of hire (salesperson and accountant in this case), you may discover that the greater cost of hiring accountants results from advertising in trade journals. If local colleges could supply your organization's needs for accountants, you could discontinue the unnecessary advertising and thereby reduce those costs.

Comparisons among recruiting sources are also useful. Table 6–1 provides a brief example of a spreadsheet with fictitious data for entry-level programmers that can be used to make such comparisons.

Applicant-tracking software or the applicant records retained by the affirmative action officer can provide the information for the first five rows of the spreadsheet. If the information is not available, the questionnaire from the

*Table 6-1*

## Recruiting Sources for Entry-Level Programmers

|  | Radio and TV Ads | Employee Referrals | Newspaper Ads | College Job Fair |
|---|---|---|---|---|
| Applicants | 84 | 27 | 157 | 29 |
| Interviews | 38 | 25 | 27 | 9 |
| Offers | 21 | 18 | 5 | 6 |
| Hires | 9 | 15 | 3 | 4 |
| Terminations, etc. (in year 1) | 4 | 2 | 1 | 1 |
| Cost paid to source | $2,300.00 | $1,500.00 | $650.00 | $4,200.00 |
| Cost per interview | $60.53 | $100.00 | $24.07 | $466.67 |
| Cost per hire | $255.56 | $100.00 | $216.67 | $1,050.00 |
| Offers/interviews | 55.26% | 72.00% | 18.52% | 66.67% |
| Hires/applicants | 10.71% | 55.56% | 1.91% | 13.79% |
| Retention rate (after year 1) | 55.56% | 86.67% | 66.67% | 75.00% |

affirmative action officer can be modified to include the following question, or newly hired employees can be asked:

> How did you learn about the position for which you are applying?
> • Radio or TV advertisement
> • Employee referral
> • Newspaper advertisement
> • College job fair

Because some applicants may feel that the answer to this question could affect the probability that they will be hired, it is recommended that the question not be asked as part of the selection-interview process. In addition, the respondents may check more than one recruiting source. In that case, the applicant should be included under each source checked, and the total number of applicants shown on the spreadsheet would be greater than the actual number of applicants. If it is important to you that each candidate identify only one source, you might ask which recruiting source had the greatest influence on the candidate's decision to apply. Once the recruiting source for each applicant has been determined, the cost paid to each recruiting source can be divided by the number of candidates interviewed to determine the cost per interview. In the same manner, to determine the cost per hire for each source, you can divide the total cost of each recruiting source by the number of candidates hired who were recruited from that recruiting source.

The number of job offers divided by the number of interviews indicates the utility of the recruiting source in filtering out the candidates before the selection interview—with the higher percentages related to more effective recruiting sources. In other words, the higher percentage indicates that you find better candidates by using that recruiting source. The number of hires divided by the number of applicants indicates the overall effectiveness of the recruiting source. This information can be especially useful in controlling the costs of recruiting. Many organizations are so eager to generate large numbers of job candidates that they fail to calculate the true cost of recruitment and may be wasting valuable resources in recruiting and screening applicants who are ill suited to the vacant positions.

The spreadsheet clearly shows that, in the fictitious example, it is much more expensive to use college job fairs than other types of recruiting sources to obtain entry-level computer programmers. A review of the spreadsheet also shows that the retention rate for employees obtained through employee referrals is higher than for the other recruitment sources. Although it appears to be one of the least expensive sources, newspaper advertising generates few hires compared to the number of applicants. If the total costs were changed to include the cost for staff time spent on such activities as screening application materials and interviewing candidates, newspaper advertising might be shown to be very expensive per hire because of the high ratio of applicants to hires.

An expansion of the spreadsheet can be used for a variety of purposes, including determining the cost per employee retained for more than 1 year and to comparing the same information for different classes of employees. Spreadsheets were designed to help answer "what if" questions very quickly. You can make changes on the spreadsheet to see the potential consequences of changes in the recruiting and hiring processes. For example, you could easily add a column for using the Internet as a recruiting source. You could also add a column to represent the totals from all of the recruiting sources and then delete the column for each recruiting source, one at a time, to estimate the overall impact on recruiting for each type of employee. When those changes are actually implemented, the relative costs and benefits of those changes can be readily determined to show the financial benefits derived from the initiatives of the HR division. You must decide how much information to include in the spreadsheet you create. It is probably best to begin with a relatively simple spreadsheet and add more items as your need for more information increases.

## Measuring Time

Time always seems to be the adversary of recruiters. New employees are needed today! There are three frequently used measures of time relative to recruitment: response time, time to fill, and time to start (Fitz-enz, 1995). Response time is the period between the date of the job requisition and the date that the first qualified candidate is referred for an interview. If you calculate this time period for all hires, you can determine your average response time by adding all your days to respond and dividing by the total hires. The following formula illustrates response time:

$$RT = RD - RR$$

where  RT is response time
RD is date of first qualified candidate referred for interview
RR is the receipt of the job requisition

Table 6–2 shows how easily the response times can be determined with a spreadsheet. As each date is entered, it is automatically converted to a number representing the day of the year, and the subtraction is performed to calculate the response times.

*Table 6–2*

## Hiring Time Lines in Days by Position

| | Review Job Description | Create Ad | Post Internally | Post Externally | Review Résumés | Interview Candidates | Make Final Offers |
|---|---|---|---|---|---|---|---|
| Accountant | 2 | 2 | 5 | 15 | 3 | 3 | 2 |
| Salesperson | 2 | 4 | 5 | 10 | 2 | 2 | 1 |
| Technician | 6 | 9 | 5 | 30 | 3 | 3 | 2 |

In this example, the tabular format of the fictitious data makes it clear that it is much more time consuming to hire technicians than other types of employees. More important, it is obvious which steps in the hiring process—reviewing the job description, creating the advertisement, and posting the job externally—need to be reviewed first.

Time to fill is the date of the job requisition minus the date on which the offer is accepted; it can be illustrated by the following formula:

$$TF = RR - OD$$

where  TF is time to fill
RR is the receipt of the job requisition
OD is the date the offer is accepted

Time to start is the date of the requisition minus the date on which the new hire starts work. It may be useful to determine other key points in the recruitment process and to record the number of elapsed days at each key point from the last event. This figure is particularly useful in determining points to consider for further evaluation to speed up the overall process. It can be helpful in explaining to others the delays that may be within their control and in identifying your unit's opportunities to improve the process. Time to start is illustrated in the following formula:

$$TS = RR - SD$$

where  TS is time until the new hire starts
RR is the receipt of the job requisition
SD is the date the new hire starts work

Further analyses can be made by creating process flow charts or spreadsheets that include the average times spent on each step of the recruitment, selection, and hiring process for each type of position. The more detailed the steps, the better you will be able to eliminate unnecessary actions and reduce the time needed for other steps in the process. Attention should be first directed toward steps that take different amounts of time because of the department or type of position. Table 6–3 summarizes data for a fictitious organization's time lines for three positions.

Another time factor that you may wish to measure is the length of time the new hire stays with the organization. Even low-cost, reduced-time recruit-

Table 6-3

## Response Times for Interviewing Candidates
(Response Time = Interview Referral Date - Recruitment Requisition Date)

| | |
|---|---|
| Average response time in days | 25 |
| Salesperson | 22 |
| Accountant | 36 |
| Clerical | 20 |

| Position | Response Time in Days | Interview Referral Date | Requisition Date |
|---|---|---|---|
| Salesperson 1 | 21 | 2/20/00 | 1/30/00 |
| Salesperson 2 | 33 | 2/27/00 | 1/25/00 |
| Salesperson 3 | 12 | 5/2/00 | 4/20/00 |
| Accountant 1 | 40 | 6/22/00 | 5/13/00 |
| Accountant 2 | 31 | 6/30/00 | 5/30/00 |
| Clerical 1 | 13 | 2/12/00 | 1/30/00 |
| Clerical 2 | 26 | 2/5/00 | 1/10/00 |

ment that must be constantly repeated is not as effective as establishing a longer term employment relationship. You will want to be creative in measuring why people stay or leave your organization. Exit interviews may provide some answers although some employees may be reticent to tell you why they are leaving, especially if there are personal reasons or climate issues within your organization that the employee believes are unlikely to change. You can measure the effects on retention of promotion, salary, benefits, incentives, and employee recognition by specific employee groupings to determine what your organization can do to retain specific groups of employees. By increasing employee retention, you can reduce turnover and the associated recruitment costs. Once again, spreadsheet analyses can help identify and compare areas of high and low turnover to determine where changes are needed.

## Conclusion
All too often, HR professionals perform their daily activities with little notice by the rest of the organization unless something goes wrong or a serious per-

sonnel problem is solved. It is increasingly important for the HR unit, like all other units in the organization, to justify its existence on the basis of the cost savings it provides the organization.

When analyzing current recruitment and hiring practices, you must determine the costs of each step in the various processes. Be sure to include the cost of meetings and committee work in your estimates. As you make improvements in your procedures, document the cost savings to the other divisions, the HR unit, and the organization. Then share the cost and labor savings with the HR staff to foster the concept of continuous improvement. Finally, discuss the cost savings with other interested parties outside the HR unit, especially with executives who can influence the allocation of financial resources.

## References and Suggested Readings

Beutell, N. J. (1996). *Instructor's manual to accompany PC projects for human resource management* (3rd ed.). Saint Paul, MN: West Publishing.

Fitz-enz, J. (1995). *How to measure human resources management* (2nd ed.). New York: McGraw-Hill.

Guion, R. M. (1998). *Assessment, measurement, and prediction for personnel decisions*. Mahwah, NJ: Lawrence Erlbaum Associates.

Schuler, R. S. (1992). *Managing human resources* (4th ed.). Saint Paul, MN: West Publishing.

Schuler, R. S., Beutell, N. J., & Youngblood, S. A. (1989). *Effective personnel management* (3rd ed.). Saint Paul, MN: West Publishing.

SHRM/CCH. (1999, June). CCH human resources management ideas and trends in personnel. *1999 SHRM/CCH survey: Recruiting practices* (Issue No. 460).

Wilson, J. B. (1999, June). *Fourteenth annual SHRM/CCH research survey: Recruitment practices*. Paper presented at the annual conference of the Society for Human Resource Management, Atlanta, GA.

# Chapter 7

# Performance Appraisal

*Daniel C. Wilson*

Performance appraisal is a formal, structured system for measuring, evaluating, and improving an employee's job-related behaviors and output. By using an effective performance appraisal system, an organization can increase its productivity, decrease nonproductive behavior, and improve its competitive status. The purpose of this chapter is to use past research in performance appraisal methodology to provide the human resource (HR) professional with a beginner's guide to creating a performance appraisal system. The author will use the fictional example of J. D. Huris, a technical training instructor working for an organization known as The Company, to illustrate the various aspects of performance appraisal.

## Uses of Performance Appraisals

Performance appraisals are used to measure each employee's contribution to meeting the needs and goals of the organization. The contribution of the individual employee, as compared to a set of standards or criteria, helps determine the relative worth of the employee's contributions as compared to the contributions of other employees in similar positions. Performance appraisals are used to provide positive or negative feedback to the employee and to assist the employee in setting new goals based on past performance. Performance appraisals are used to motivate employees to improve their performance by tying performance to rewards such as recognition, gifts, bonuses, merit increases, compensation, and opportunities for promotions.

Performance appraisals are also used for staff development and HR planning. Past performance is recognized as a predictor of future performance. In addition, the dialogue accompanying performance appraisals can help determine how each employee's career goals fit with the needs of the organization.

Therefore, performance appraisals can be used to identify employees who have demonstrated the potential ability to accept positions of increased responsibility and to match employees and positions according to the individuals' abilities and career goals. The organization can then compare the present supply of qualified employees with the projected needs for each position and take appropriate measures to ensure that all openings are filled in a timely and effective manner.

Valid performance appraisals serve as a basis for making other HR decisions such as promotions, demotions, rewards, punishments, and terminations. HR decisions based on measured performance are highly defensible in legal actions against the organization that stem from charges of discrimination, illegal termination, and so forth. The performance appraisals serve as a record to document the rationale for past decisions.

A summary of the uses of performance appraisals follows:

- Measure employee's contribution to company goals
- Determine the relative worth of the employee's contribution
- Provide feedback to the employee
- Motivate the employee
- Improve individual and team performance
- Provide the basis for rewards and recognition
- Promote staff development and career planning
- Contribute to HR planning
- Inform promotions, demotions, transfers, and terminations
- Serve as documentation for legal defense

## J. D. Huris

The Company has established a recognition program for outstanding performance that includes gifts and merit increases. The recipients of both rewards are selected on the basis of their performance evaluations. However, the selection process is not competitive, and each employee's performance is judged against a known set of standards rather than compared to the performance of other employees. In the event that the technical training instructor, J. D. Huris, does not meet the minimum performance standards for continued employment, the unsatisfactory performance evaluations would serve as the documentation justifying the termination.

There are three levels of technical training instructor at The Company. J. D. is at level 1, the lowest level. As part of J. D.'s performance evaluation, the supervisor would use an organization chart to show the most likely career paths available to J. D.

The supervisor and the HR staff could use the information from the collective performance evaluations of J. D. and other level 1 technical training instructors to estimate the time needed for an entry-level employee to get ready for the responsibilities of level 2 and to determine the number of "level 1s" who are ready for promotion to level 2. This information could then be used as part of the HR staff-planning database.

## Creating an Effective Performance Appraisal System

An effective performance appraisal system begins with identifying the goals of the organization and determining how the performance of each employee contributes to meeting those goals. This task is accomplished in part by relating the organization's mission and goals to departmental goals. From the departmental goals, performance outcomes can be determined for the employees as a group. The next step involves conducting job analyses to determine the job duties and responsibilities for each employee and creating appropriate job descriptions. A job analysis is the procedure for gathering information about the work performed, the physical requirements, the knowledge and skill requirements, the working environment or conditions, the machinery and equipment used, and the performance standards related to a specific job. This information is gathered through direct observation of incumbents, interviews with incumbents and supervisors, questionnaires, and work logs. Job descriptions are a direct result of the job analyses and contain much of the same information, which is written in a consistent format.

### Job Descriptions

Job descriptions have already been developed for most organizations and need to be revised only to reflect the current and future needs of the organization and the various departments. Job descriptions can be created with minimal effort by using software such as that produced by G. Neil Companies and Descriptions Now! by KnowledgePoint. From the job descriptions, additional performance criteria can be established, and performance outcomes can be determined for each employee.

Often, managers and others responsible for conducting performance appraisals give attention to the appraisal process only at the end of the appraisal period, just before the performance appraisals are to be completed. However, if the employees are to strive to achieve their goals, they need to know what the goals are before they begin. The performance criteria and outcomes should be communicated in specific terms to each employee at the beginning of the performance appraisal period so the employee clearly understands his or her goals and objectives. Job descriptions can be used to create a logical order and format for conveying that information to the employee.

## J. D. Huris

The Company has the following mission statement: to provide the highest possible customer service throughout the organization. The Commercial Sales Division has the following mission statement: to provide the highest possible service to all of The Company's customers—past, present, and future. One of the goals of the division is to provide prompt and efficient training in the use and routine maintenance of machinery sold by The Company. Because the Commercial Sales Division sells complex equipment, it depends on the technical training instructors to teach the customers about the use of the equipment. The more the customers know about the machinery that they have purchased, the more satisfied they tend to be with the machinery and The Company. The contribution of J. D. Huris is very closely tied to the goals of the division and the organization.

A job description for technical training instructors was created from a recent job analysis. The description includes the job title, a summary, the essential duties and responsibilities, the work environment, and the job specifications or qualifications needed to perform the job. To illustrate the general design, a partial job description was created using Descriptions Now! by KnowledgePoint (see Figure 7–1).

## Formative and Summative Evaluations

Job descriptions can also be used to create feedback systems relating to job performance. Employees need ongoing feedback to measure their progress toward the goals and objectives established at the beginning of the appraisal period. Formative evaluations are a means by which employees can obtain information about their progress. Formative evaluations have several advantages. They aid in project management by helping each employee determine if he or she is meeting the time lines for each step of the project. They help employees and managers determine if quality standards are being met on an ongoing basis. If outcomes are used as part of the performance evaluation measures, formative evaluations can include information about when, in what quantity, and to what

*Figure 7-1*————————————————————————————

# Sample Job Description

The Company
Job Description

Job Title: Technical Training Instructor
Department:
Reports to:
FLSA Status:
Prepared by:
Prepared Date:
Approved by:
Approved Date:

**Summary:** Develops and conducts programs to train employees or customers of industrial or commercial establishments in installation, programming, safety, maintenance, and repair of machinery.

**Essential Duties and Responsibilities:** Performs the following duties. Other duties may be assigned.

- Confers with management and staff or Technical Training Coordinator to determine training objectives.

- Writes training program (including outline, text, handouts, and tests) and designs laboratory exercises.

- Schedules classes according to classroom and equipment availability.

- Lectures class on safety, installation, programming, maintenance, and repair of machinery and equipment, following program outline, hand outs, and texts.

- Demonstrates procedures being taught, such as programming and repair. Observes trainees in laboratory and answers trainees' questions.

**Continued on page 82**

Continued from page 81

- Administers written and practical exams, and writes performance reports to evaluate trainees' performance.

- Participates in meetings, seminars, and training sessions to obtain information useful to training facility and integrates information into training program.

---

quality standards outcomes were achieved. Formative evaluations also minimize the effect of primacy and recency types of evaluation errors by providing a record of each employee's performance and outcomes throughout the performance evaluation period.

In many organizations, summative evaluations are synonymous with the performance appraisal. They are completed at the end of the performance appraisal period. When formative evaluations are used, the summative evaluations are easily done, and the results should come as no surprise to the evaluator or to the employee being evaluated. As the name implies, summative evaluations are merely summaries of the preceding performance period. An advantage of summative evaluations is that, unlike formative evaluations, which focus on isolated behaviors and outcomes within short time frames, they can help employees see how their behavior over a longer period of time contributes to the success of their department and the organization. Summative evaluations also provide a composite overview that includes how each employee performed during the evaluation period, under what conditions the employee worked, what the employee accomplished, what the employee needs from management, and what the employee needs to do to improve his or her performance. In addition, summative evaluations serve as the basis for establishing the goals and objectives of each employee for the next performance evaluation period.

Summative evaluations also have one more use. The summative evaluations from several performance appraisal periods can be used as though they were formative evaluations conducted over a long period of time. The collection of these summative evaluations can then be used to justify HR decisions related to promotions, transfers, and so forth, and can be especially useful in making decisions about upper management positions.

## J. D. Huris

When J. D. first started with The Company, an experienced technical training instructor was asked to serve as a mentor. The mentor reviewed J. D.'s lesson plans, observed two of the lessons he presented, and provided written as well as oral feedback about J. D.'s performance. In addition, J. D. completed a self-appraisal each week and used it to identify strengths and weaknesses in the lessons; determine the information, supplies, or equipment needed to present better training; and record comments and suggestions made by the students.

J. D. no longer has a mentor, but he continues to complete self-appraisals and meets with the supervisor on a quarterly basis. To continually improve the quality of instruction that J. D. provides, J. D. and the supervisor review the same items as when J. D. first began. J. D. hopes to become a technical training coordinator, and the discussions also include career planning and progress reviews.

On the anniversary of J. D.'s employment with The Company, J. D. and the supervisor complete summary evaluations. These performance evaluations are a detailed summary of J. D.'s performance throughout the preceding year. They include the number of training programs created and presented, the number of students served, and the number of training "graduates." Because training provided to customers has been shown (by use of the correlation coefficient) to be closely related to repeat sales, a cost-benefit analysis for the training programs is used as another performance measure. The cost is the dollar value of the supplies, equipment, and rooms and J. D.'s compensation required to complete a training program. The benefit is the repeat sales to the customer following the training. J. D. has expressed concern about this measurement because repeat sales are dependent on several other variables, including the state of the economy, the needs of the customer, the financial strength of the customer, and changes in the machinery produced by The Company.

## What to Evaluate

Many appraisal methods are somewhat subjective because human biases cannot be completely eliminated. However, by selecting the right things to measure, it is possible to increase the objectivity, establish validity, and maximize the utility of the performance appraisal process. Important job duties and responsibilities identified through the job analyses can be further detailed into related tasks and can serve as the basis for establishing performance criteria. In addition, tasks related to special projects can be identified. Finally, because it is appropriate to measure the results of an employee's efforts, outcomes can be used. It is time consuming to create performance evaluation systems that include all of the tasks and outcomes associated with each job description and special project. As a result, many performance appraisal forms summarize related types of behavior and leave space for the evaluator to make comments, thereby providing some of the detail lacking in the form. However, it is beneficial to establish performance standards for each of the important tasks. Performance standards can be established only if each one of the tasks is identified and if tasks are not lost by being summarized as duties.

### J. D. Huris

A few of the essential duties included in the job description for the technical training instructor are as follows:

- Write training programs
- Schedule classes
- Present lessons
- Administer examinations

A performance evaluation based on only the duties would be vague as to what performance was being evaluated. The result could be misinterpretation of the evaluation, less than ideal communication, and mistrust between the supervisor and J. D. Huris.

By contrast, the following list includes the duties and related tasks from the job description:

- Write training programs
  - Write lesson plan outlines
  - Create lecture notes
  - Prepare handouts
  - Create written examinations
  - Design hands-on exercises
  - Design practical examinations
- Schedule classes
  - Determine the location of classes (at The Company or at the customer's location)
  - Determine the number of students
  - Determine when the students are available for training
  - Reserve classrooms and laboratory rooms
  - Reserve equipment for training

- Present lessons
  - Present lectures
  - Explain safety precautions
  - Demonstrate proper operation of machinery
  - Demonstrate routine maintenance procedures
- Administer examinations
  - Proctor written examinations
  - Observe practical examinations
  - Evaluate students' performance

If the performance evaluation form includes each of the tasks listed above, there will be little doubt about what performance is being evaluated. The extra detail enhances the meaning and value of the performance appraisal.

The importance of each task depends on the frequency with which it must be performed and the consequences associated with its satisfactory or unsatisfactory completion. A task that has a large effect on the organization or unit should be weighted according to consequences to the organization that are associated with performance of that task. If each duty and task are weighted, a more accurate reflection of the employee's performance will result. The overall performance evaluation becomes a weighted measurement that is directly related to the goals of the organization and unit.

### J. D. Huris

Comments from the customers (i.e., students) of The Company indicate that most of them do not want examinations as part of the training program. But liability concerns mean The Company and its customers need to have some assurance that the persons operating the machinery know how to operate it safely. Both of those factors affect the performance evaluation of J. D. Huris. J. D. is still expected to administer written and practical examinations related to safety. However, because examinations are not part of other training lessons, the weight given to the preparation and administration of examinations is less than for other tasks.

## Establishing Performance Standards

Standards of performance may have been determined for most of the routine tasks performed by each employee. The standards may be the result of contract negotiations, may be taken from accepted professional and trade association standards, or may be developed over time within the organization. For special projects or new tasks (often the result of changes in technology and production methods) standards will need to be established. At first, those standards are based on the collective judgment of management and incumbents, and later they are based on the experience of the organization.

## J. D. Huris

The goals of the organizational unit should first be used to develop performance standards for the duty and tasks. For example, research may have shown that customers are satisfied with the service when training programs are delivered within 6 days. The minimum speed standard for delivering training programs might be to respond to 80% of the requests for training within 6 days, and the goal might be to answer 80% of the requests within 2 days. A scale for measuring the employee's performance is then easily created. Determining the measurement standard for providing an appropriate written examination might be even simpler. If a standard written examination format is to be used, the minimum acceptable performance level is that all written examinations include between 40 and 60 true/false and multiple-choice questions. Anything shorter or longer than the standard range is unacceptable. How are measurement standards created, however, for the task of creating complete and accurate written examinations? Written examinations created for other training programs could serve as the standard. Customers and experienced technical training instructors have been able to judge the appropriateness of the length and format of the previously administered examinations. The examinations created by J. D. Huris would provide an indisputable record of the completeness, accuracy, and format of the examinations. Each of the exams could be rated on those criteria.

## The Appraisal Instrument

The most common performance appraisal instruments are the straight ranking, alternation ranking, forced distribution, graphic rating scale, critical incident method, behaviorally anchored rating scales (BARS), behavior observation scale (BOS), direct index, and management by objectives (MBO). The first three approaches are norm referenced. They measure the relative performance of the individual employee against the performance of other employees in the same or similar positions. These ranking approaches are based on objective criteria, are relatively simple to use, and avoid the bias toward central tendency. However, if the employees' performance levels are very similar, these rankings can create a false depiction of the performance of the individual employee. Using the two extremes, if all of the employees are performing at very low levels, the ranking may lead the top performers to believe that their performance is satisfactory simply because it is better than the performance of their peers. By contrast, if all of the employees are performing at very high levels, the lowest ranked employees may justifiably believe that they have been evaluated unfairly.

The critical incident evaluation method involves the use of narrative to describe the employee's behaviors that had either a very positive or very negative consequence. Graphic rating scales and BARS measure an employee's absolute performance on critical behaviors related to the job duties. On the graphic rating scale, the evaluator is free to define the behavior as well as to assign a numerical value to the quality of performance. The graphic rating scale is simple to create, but it lacks definition and clarity. The BARS approach uses critical incident or behavior statements that illustrate poor, average, or outstanding performance that are grouped by dimensions of job-related work. The employee's performance is given a numerical score on the basis of the statement that best describes his or her behavior on the given work dimension. The BARS approach is far more accurate than the graphic rating scale, but it takes a great amount of time to develop and the performance evaluation is centered on processes rather than outcomes. One of the major problems associated with graphic rating scales and BARS stems from grouping behaviors before assigning a rating. With the former scale, the groupings are vague. With the latter, the groupings may mean that an employee who performs well on one behavior and poorly on another would receive a meaningless "average" score for that work dimension.

The BOS performance evaluation method also relies on direct observation of the employee's performance of job-related behaviors, positive or negative. However, instead of measuring the level of performance, the evaluator measures the frequency of the behavior. The obvious difficulty with the BOS approach is that evaluators seldom have the opportunity to accurately determine the frequency of the employee's behavior.

The direct index approach to performance evaluation measures objective criteria such as the number of acceptable units produced, the dollar value of sales, the number of absences, and the number of customer complaints. By starting with the goals and objectives of the organization, conducting job analyses, and creating comprehensive lists of job-related tasks, one can include in the performance evaluation important job-related behaviors. The objectives established for the individual employee are not based entirely on behaviors, however; instead, they are based on the outcomes related to those behaviors. When the direct index approach is used to evaluate managers, their performance evaluations are dependent on the behaviors and, more importantly, the output of their subordinates. With the direct index approach, the goals and objectives of the employee are established by the supervisor or his or her superiors.

An alternative approach to goal setting is used in the MBO approach. MBO performance evaluation begins with the supervisor or evaluator and the employee working together to establish the employee's goals and objectives for the performance evaluation period. Then strategies for reaching the goals are developed. The next step is to evaluate the employee's performance by measuring it against the previously established goals. Finally, new goals and objectives are set for the upcoming performance evaluation period by using the current performance evaluation as a base.

### Sample Performance Appraisals

Figures 7–2, 7–3, and 7–4 illustrate various types of performance appraisals as applied to the duties and tasks of J. D. Huris's job description. The norm-referenced appraisals are self-explanatory and are not included.

*Figure 7-2*————————————————————————

# Sample Performance Appraisal

### Graphic Rating Scale Performance Appraisal

Instructions:
Carefully evaluate employee's work performance in relation to current job requirements. Circle the rating letter to indicate the employee's performance. Assign points for each rating within the scale. Total and average the points to provide an overall performance score.

### Rating Definitions
**S**—Superior Performance is exceptional in every respect, clearly far better than is expected.

**AA**—Above Average Performance is of a high quality and quantity. Employee exceeds most requirements on a regular basis.

**A**—Average Performance is consistently satisfactory. Employee exceeds minimum requirements. **Continued on page 89**

Continued from page 88

**NI**—Needs Improvement Performance is less than satisfactory in some aspects. Employee occasionally does not meet minimum standards.

**U**—Unsatisfactory Performance does not meet minimum standards. Continued performance at this level could lead to termination.

| Criteria | Rating | | Comments |
|---|---|---|---|
| **Quality**—accuracy, completeness | S | 4 | _____ |
| | AA | 3 | _____ |
| | A | 2 | _____ |
| | NI | 1 | _____ |
| | U | 0 | _____ |
| **Quantity**—amount of work completed in a given period of time | S | 4 | _____ |
| | AA | 3 | _____ |
| | A | 2 | _____ |
| | NI | 1 | _____ |
| | U | 0 | _____ |
| **Reliability**—consistency of work | S | 4 | _____ |
| | AA | 3 | _____ |
| | A | 2 | _____ |
| | NI | 1 | _____ |
| | U | 0 | _____ |
| **Dependability**—punctuality, lack of absences, observance of work rules | S | 4 | _____ |
| | AA | 3 | _____ |
| | A | 2 | _____ |
| | NI | 1 | _____ |
| | U | 0 | _____ |
| **Initiative**—work performed with no or little direction or supervision | S | 4 | _____ |
| | AA | 3 | _____ |
| | A | 2 | _____ |
| | NI | 1 | _____ |
| | U | 0 | _____ |

*Figure 7-3*—————————————————————————

## Sample Performance Appraisal

**Behaviorally Anchored Rating Scale for the Duty—Presents Lecture**

**8** Presents complete illustrated lectures with PowerPoint slides, demonstrations, and examples

**7** Presents complete illustrated lectures with PowerPoint slides and examples

**6** Presents complete illustrated lectures with PowerPoint slides

**5** Presents lectures by using the chalkboard to illustrate points

**4** Presents lectures that draw positive comments from students

**3** Presents lectures that thoroughly cover the subject matter

**2** Presents lectures that include some examples

**1** Presents lectures without reading notes

---

## Establishing Validity

One purpose of determining what to evaluate, how to weight each item, and how to measure the quality of performance is to develop a performance appraisal system that measures job performance and outcomes—but nothing else. In measurement terminology, this system is known as validity. In other words, validity is an instrument or system that measures what it purports to measure. Several types of validity can be used in the performance appraisal process. Construct validity is used to measure a construct or trait such as leadership or intelligence. Measurement of traits is not recommended for performance appraisals because it is difficult to demonstrate that the trait is actually being measured by the appraisal, and it is also difficult to prove that the trait is directly related to job performance. Content validity is the degree to which a measurement device that includes only a sampling of work measures the intended job performance. It is established by using a sampling of the work performed by incumbents on

*Figure 7-4*

## Sample Performance Appraisal

### Behavioral Observation Scale

With **0** being Never and **4** being Always, circle the number that indicates how often the employee exhibits each of the following behaviors.

| | |
|---|---|
| Criticizes students in front of class | **0  1  2  3  4** |
| Calls on students by name | **0  1  2  3  4** |
| Praises students in front of class | **0  1  2  3  4** |
| | |
| Uses examples to enhance the lecture | **0  1  2  3  4** |
| Provides illustrations to enhance the lecture | **0  1  2  3  4** |
| Demonstrates proper use of machinery | **0  1  2  3  4** |
| Explains safety precautions | **0  1  2  3  4** |
| Demonstrates proper maintenance procedures | **0  1  2  3  4** |
| | |
| Carefully observes students during written exams | **0  1  2  3  4** |
| Carefully observes students during practical exams | **0  1  2  3  4** |
| Evaluates students' performance on exams in a timely manner | **0  1  2  3  4** |
| Fails to return written exams by the next lesson | **0  1  2  3  4** |

a regular basis. This type of validity would be used if the HR practitioner wanted to create a performance appraisal form that covered the full range of job performance—with sample elements used to measure each aspect of the job. Predictive validity is the degree to which a device can predict how well an individual will do in the future. Examples of this type are college entrance examinations that are used to predict success in college course work and leadership aptitude tests used to select supervisors in an organization. If past performance appraisals are used for promotions, the predictive validity for the appraisals needs to be established.

HR professionals probably already keep records of the various employment test scores of successful applicants and the performance evaluation scores of employees. In divisions in which sufficient numbers of new hires and promotions occur, it is possible to determine the validity coefficients and regression coefficients of each selection method. This information and the average cost of each selection method allow the HR professionals to determine the relative utility of each method. If there are steps in the selection process that are not valid because they neither relate to nor predict future job performance, they should be eliminated. Invalid steps add to costs and are indefensible in a discrimination suit.

It is important to ensure that the appraisal system measures performance and outcomes. Personality traits should not be evaluated. Terms such as dependability, initiative, and responsibility should be avoided when creating performance appraisal systems. Credibility and legal problems can arise when subjective judgments are simply turned into numbers in an effort to present them as objective measurement. It is better to measure individual, observable behaviors rather than summarize a group of behaviors in terms of a personality trait or characteristic. Supervisors often find the critical incidents method useful in noting observable behaviors. In this method, they keep information in a file or computer on work incidents for each employee. They document comments from customers on excellent service and serious employee errors, including the consequences of the employee's actions.

## Establishing Reliability

Measuring the right things (i.e., validity) is necessary but not sufficient for a sound performance appraisal system. It is also important to ensure consistency in evaluation, a measurement concept referred to as reliability. A performance evaluation system must provide the same results from one evaluator or rater to the next and from one employee to the next in order to be useful and legally defensible. As previously noted, one technique for creating a reliable performance evaluation system is to evaluate only observable behaviors. The measurement techniques should also make clear distinctions between the levels of performance, from unacceptable to acceptable to outstanding. Performance appraisal forms should use specific, commonly understood terms to describe behavior that leave little room for interpretation by the evaluators. For example, in rating the timeliness with which an employee completed assignments, words such as "unacceptable," "satisfactory," and "excellent" should be replaced with phrases such as "Completed—1 or more days after the due date, on the due date, 1 or more days before the due date."

Another technique for increasing validity and reliability involves the careful selection of evaluators. An immediate supervisor is often the single evaluator of an employee's performance. To increase the reliability of the ratings completed by the supervisor, the supervisor needs to be familiar with the tasks performed by the employee. Supervisors who have been promoted from within usually have the greatest knowledge about the tasks performed by their subordinates because those supervisors performed the same tasks before being promoted. The supervisor also needs firsthand knowledge of the employee's performance. That knowledge can come from direct observation of the employee or from a direct interest in the outcomes of the performance.

Appraisals by subordinates have some of the same advantages as ratings by supervisors. Although the subordinates may not have as much knowledge about the supervisor's tasks as in the reverse situation, they often have opportunities to observe the supervisor's behaviors from a unique perspective. In addition, because each supervisor usually has several subordinates, it is much easier to determine whether the performance evaluations are consistent from one subordinate to the next (i.e., interrater reliability).

When employees work together as teams, they can conduct performance evaluations on each other. Although peer evaluations may suffer from a leniency type of bias, they tend to be consistent from one evaluation period to the next for established teams. Formative evaluations of this type are useful not only in evaluating the performance of each employee but also in measuring the progress of the team in reaching a goal or completing a project. They also help team members recognize the value of diversity, and they may help teams reassign tasks to individual employees on the basis of the strengths and weaknesses of each team member.

The validity and reliability of the ratings from each of the previously mentioned groups can be increased by training in conducting performance appraisals. Supervisors need to know how to set goals and objectives, in cooperation with each employee, that meet the needs of the organization. Peers and subordinates will have little opportunity to set goals for other employees, but they need to know what the evaluated employee's goals were and how the goals were set. Evaluators also need to know how to measure the employee's performance against his or her goals for evaluation period. Training is also needed to help raters avoid errors related to negative bias, leniency, primacy and recency, and central tendency.

Customer appraisals are appropriate to measure performance on tasks that are observed only by customers. However, customers are not trained in performance evaluation methods, and the ratings may suffer from a negative bias. Customers often focus on poor performance resulting in customer dissatisfaction. Customers may also believe excellent performance constitutes the minimal acceptable level of performance. It may appear that customer appraisals are more useful in setting the goals and objectives of the organization or for changing customer service processes than for evaluating the performance of individual employees. However, it is the performance of each employee that determines the value added to the product or service provided to the customer.

When the employees evaluated are expatriates, the selection of the appropriate evaluators is even more important. According to Hill (2000), "most expatriates appear to believe more weight should be given to an on-site manager's appraisal than to an off-site manager's appraisal." The on-site evaluator is more likely to have firsthand knowledge of the employee's performance. However, if the evaluator and the employee are from different cultures, the evaluation may be negatively biased because of cultural differences. Regardless of whether the evaluator is a superior, subordinate, peer, or customer, such biases are less likely to occur if the evaluator is of the same nationality as the employee. Many times, especially in upper management positions, the supervisor of the employee is located at the organization's headquarters. In those circumstances, the supervisor can perform the appraisals in consultation with a group of persons that includes former expatriates to the same foreign assignment, on-site subordinates, peers, and so forth.

A relatively new approach is the 360-degree appraisal. The biases inherent in any one of the sources mentioned earlier are reduced by using a combination of superiors, peers, subordinates, and internal and external customers as evaluators. This appraisal system is based on the assumption that more evaluators lead to greater knowledge of the employee's performance, greater diversity of the evaluators, and a more accurate evaluation. Suggestions for enhancing the validity and reliability of the 360-degree appraisal include protecting the anonymity of the raters and using a combination of peers, subordinates, superiors, and customers.

### J. D. Huris

J. D. Huris and several level 1 co-workers are being considered for promotion to the position of level 2 technical training instructor. In the following example, past performance appraisal scores and written test scores are used to predict job performance in the level 2 position. By using some elementary statistical analysis and the power of the computer, the HR practitioner can determine the validity of these two selection procedures.

Nearly all spreadsheet software includes built-in statistical formulas. The help menus really do help the novice user of statistics create spreadsheets that will take full advantage of the power of statistics to make reasonable decisions about the use of various employee recruiting and selection methods.

Beutell (1996) provides formulas and spreadsheet examples in textbook and diskette form for determining the validity coefficients and regression coefficients for two common selection methods used to hire new employees and to choose among persons eligible for promotion: the employment test and past-performance evaluation scores.

In the examples provided by Beutell, the results of the two validity coefficients show the past-performance scores to be more valid because they produce the higher positive number and are, therefore, more effective as an employee selection method. To calculate the validity coefficient for any other selection methods, simply substitute the scores of the new selection method for the test scores and the interview scores.

A formula for calculating the estimated present dollar value of replacing one selection procedure with another can be found in works by Beutell (1996) and by Jackson and Schuler (2000). In the example provided by Beutell, the present dollar value of using past-performance evaluation scores instead of an employment test to select employees for promotion is nearly $300,000. Obviously, the results for a particular organization would be different, but the principle is the same. Although the formula is complex, it is relatively simple to enter into a spreadsheet, and it can be used with little modification for many selection methods and many groups of employees. It also provides a means to demonstrate, in estimated present value dollars, the advantage of retaining some selection methods and discontinuing others. The use of this type of formula may help overcome the desire by some persons to use employee selection methods that are no longer useful, and it can justify the use of more effective selection methods.

## Conclusion

No single performance appraisal method is suitable for all types of positions. A variety of performance appraisal methods allow an organization to guide, motivate, and structure its workforce to achieve a competitive advantage based on its human resources. The HR staff can design performance evaluation forms, train evaluators, collect and analyze information from performance appraisals, and create a performance appraisal system to meet the needs of the employees and achieve the goals of the organization. By taking the extra step to calculate the dollar utility of performance appraisals, the HR staff can truly contribute to the bottom line.

## References and Suggested Readings

Adler, R. L., & Coleman, T. (1999, April). Performance management profile: Example audit of an HR function [46 paragraphs] (SHRM White Paper). [On-line]. Available: <http://www.shrm.org/whitepapers/documents/61123.asp>.

Beutell, N. J. (1996). *Instructor's manual to accompany PC projects for human resource management* (3rd ed.). St. Paul, MN: West Publishing.

Descriptions Now! [Computer software]. (1997). Pentaluma, CA: KnowledgePoint.

Dessler, G. (2000). *Human resource management* (8th ed.). Upper Saddle River, NJ: Prentice-Hall.

Employer's toolbox [Human resource forms and tip sheets]. (1998). Sunrise, FL: G. Neil.

Fox, J. F. (1997). Performance appraisal. In R. Kaufman, S. Thiagarajan, P. MacGillis (Eds.), *The guidebook for performance improvement: Working with individuals and organizations* (pp. 601–615). San Francisco: Jossey-Bass Pfeiffer.

Hill, C. W. L. (2000). *International business: Competing in the global marketplace* (3rd ed.). Boston: McGraw Hill.

Jackson, S. E., & Schuler, R. S. (2000). *Managing human resources: A partnership perspective* (7th ed.). Cincinnati, OH: South-Western College Publishing.

Janes, S. T. (1994). Selecting trainees. In W. R. Tracey (Ed.), *Human resources management and development handbook* (2nd ed.) (pp. 1263–1269). New York: AMACOM.

Mathis, R. L., & Jackson, J. H. (1988). *Personnel/human resource management* (5th ed.). St. Paul, MN: West Publishing.

Pardue, H. M. (1999, May). Performance appraisal as an employee development tool [41 paragraphs] (SHRM White Paper). [On-line]. Available: <http://www.shrm.org/whitepapers/ documents/61610.asp>.

Performance Now! [Computer software]. (1997). Pentaluma, CA: KnowledgePoint.

## Chapter 8

# Making 360-Degree Feedback Work for Your Organization

*Sara Brown*

Three-hundred-and-sixty-degree feedback, sometimes called multirater or multisource feedback, is a process through which individuals (i.e., participants) receive feedback from others (i.e., raters)—typically their supervisor, peers, subordinates, and sometimes customers—with whom good working relationships are key to a participant's effectiveness. Not only does this process identify areas for improvement and development, but it also serves to reinforce and affirm an individual's strengths. (Many participants report that the feedback that they receive from a 360-degree process far exceeds the quality and depth of feedback that they would receive through ordinary means in their organizations.)

## The Issue of Trust

Trust is a crucial issue if an organization is considering the use of 360-degree feedback. A 360-degree program is doomed to failure if prospective participants and raters do not trust the organization's intentions in offering (or requiring) their participation. If participants fear that the feedback will be used against them in some way, they are likely to resist being involved. Therefore, before embarking on a 360-degree feedback process, an organization must do some soul-searching on the issue of trust. Will participants and raters trust that feedback will remain confidential and anonymous? If they have doubts, the HR professional may need to do some trust building before proceeding.

Ideally, confidentiality and anonymity wouldn't be necessary—one could just invite one's supervisor, subordinates, and peers into a room and ask for their feedback. But most individuals aren't that thick-skinned, and the culture of most organizations isn't that open to feedback even if trust is reasonably high among staff. For that reason, many organizations using 360-degree feedback opt for methods that protect the anonymity of raters, particularly when the raters are subordinates. By doing so, organizations avoid even subtle repercussions from participants and increase the likelihood of raters' candor.

## Purpose of 360-Degree Feedback

An organization considering 360-degree feedback must decide how the feedback will be used. Typically, it is used for individual professional development, performance appraisals (or some combination of the two), the identification of training needs, or the determination of the organization's ability to achieve its strategic goals by relying on its current level of employee talent.

Ultimately, the purpose of 360-degree feedback is to improve performance. Whether the feedback is used for development or appraisal purposes, the process is most valuable to the organization if the behaviors measured for individuals are linked to strategic goals. The strategic goals may be either broad, organizationwide goals or narrower goals for a given department. For example, entrepreneurial behavior may be an important organizationwide goal, while effective peer relations may be critical in a particular department.

One approach to determining what should be measured is to engage managers in a discussion about the behavioral competencies (i.e., observable values, beliefs, and skills associated with superior performance) that will be required of leaders or staff to accomplish the strategic goals. Once the necessary competencies have been identified, the consolidated feedback from all participants can be used to determine to what extent the organization has the capacity to achieve its goals. Also, this consolidated feedback helps identify the organization's most pressing training needs.

## Gathering Data

Developing an assessment inventory requires expertise that many organizations do not have in house. For example, it is critical to identify the skills and competencies for 360-degree assessment that a participant could learn and develop. Also, the competencies that are identified must be those that will make a difference in the organization and lead to the accomplishment of the organization's strategic purpose. The competencies used for development might be more general than those used for an individual's performance appraisal (the results of which might be used for pay, promotion, or demotion decisions). But regardless of what they are used for, competency statements must be written in unambiguous behavioral language (i.e., a clear statement of the participant's behavior that a rater might have observed).

Therefore, once HR professionals know what observable behavior they want to measure in the 360-degree feedback process, they will have to decide whether to create their own inventory, use an "off the shelf" inventory, or use the services of a consultant to help them customize an inventory. The objective is to find or create an inventory as closely aligned as possible to the competencies needed in an organization to achieve strategic goals.

## Choosing an Inventory

If the HR professional decides to purchase an inventory, there are a number of good 360-degree products on the market. The April 1999 *Training and Development* magazine reviews 10 of those products on the basis of factors such as

- Assessment purpose
- Target audience
- Number of items
- Validity
- Data collection options
- Location of scoring (i.e., vendor or client location)
- Appearance and insightfulness of results
- Customization options
- Price

Because completing and scoring the inventories is a time-consuming process, many vendors are shifting from paper-and-pencil data collection to electronic means—web site, e-mail, disk, or fax. The Otis Elevator Company provides a good example of electronic data collection (see the May 1999 *HRMagazine*). By using a web site, raters at Otis were able to quickly and effectively provide confidential management development feedback.

## Confidentiality and Anonymity

Although an Internet-based method of data collection speeds up the process, particularly for those raters who have been asked to provide feedback for several individuals, the most important factor is whether the process will provide objectivity for the participant and confidentiality and anonymity for the raters. If it does not, the results will be suspect and the response rate will be low. For that reason, organizations often use a third-party source (i.e., a vendor or consultant) to process the data and prepare reports.

## Selecting Participants and Raters

A rule of thumb for selecting participants for 360-degree feedback is to choose individuals who have been in their current jobs for a minimum of 6 months or, preferably, a year. The same is true for those persons selected to be raters. To fairly observe the behavior of a participant, prospective raters should have been in a position to make observations for at least 6 months and preferably longer.

The most typical complement of raters is (a) self (i.e., the participant's self-rating), (b) supervisor, (c) subordinates, and (d) peers. A minimum of three subordinates and three peers should be selected—and preferably more in case someone fails to respond.

Who should be chosen to be a rater, and who should do the choosing? Following are several strategies that an organization might consider:

- Aim for a balanced perspective. Choose a mixed slate of raters, some of whom are likely to be positive and some negative.
- Aim for high-impact feedback. Choose the individuals most critical to the participant's success even though they may not be complimentary raters.
- Aim for inclusion. Ask all of a participant's subordinates to provide feedback in order to get a comprehensive overview and to avoid the perception of favoritism.
- Select peers who have ongoing work relationships with the participant. Choose members of operating committees, team members, and individuals from other departments with whom the participant works closely rather than literal peers on the organization chart.

Who should choose the raters? Companies handle the selection differently. Some ask the participants to choose the raters; other companies prefer that the decision be made collaboratively between the participants and their supervisors.

## Training Participants and Raters

If 360-degree feedback is new to the organization or the department in which it will be used, it is important to communicate its "big picture" purpose before initiating training. Everybody in the organization (whether or not they have been chosen to be participants or raters) will want answers to these questions: How will 360-degree feedback benefit the company and the individuals receiving it? What decisions, if any, will be based on the feedback? What groups of people will receive the feedback? How will participants be chosen? Will other groups have an opportunity to participate at a later time?

There are three groups in particular that need training as part of their introduction to 360-degree feedback: the participants, the raters, and the participants' supervisors. All three groups need to understand the meaning of the rating scales (e.g., range of responses from "strongly disagree" to "strongly agree" and when it is appropriate to respond "don't know"). Raters need to understand the importance and value of the feedback to the participants and, therefore, to take seriously their responsibility as raters. Raters who have been asked to respond to more than one participant must be sure to respond within the context of each participant's job and not compare one participant to another. If the 360-degree feedback form invites a narrative response, raters should be encouraged to respond constructively.

Because the responses of supervisors are often revealed to the participant and not grouped with the peer responses, supervisors must be prepared to candidly discuss their ratings with participants. (It is helpful if supervisors keep copies of their responses so they are prepared to discuss them.) Also, if the feedback is to be used for developmental purposes and not for performance review, the supervisor's role must be clarified as that of a coach.

Training for participants should include a discussion of how feedback facilitates career growth and of strategies for receiving feedback. One such strategy is to administer a personality profile to participants, such as the Myers-Briggs Type Indicator (MBTI), Birkman, FIRO-B, or one of the DISC inventories produced by companies such as Carlson Learning or Target Training International. A personality profile gives participants an additional framework within which to consider and objectify the feedback that they receive. For example, if a participant took the MBTI and learned that he or she had a strong preference for gaining all possible information before making a decision (an MBTI "P"), that individual might not be surprised to get feedback indicating that others see him or her as indecisive.

## Planning for Change

An organization may have chosen or developed a carefully crafted 360-degree inventory and used sophisticated, electronic means of collecting the data, but if participants (a) do not trust the results, (b) cannot interpret the report, and (c) do not believe the results are relevant to them, the organization has wasted a lot of time and money. To avoid those problems,

• Establish trust. Be scrupulous in protecting the confidentiality of the data collection process and the appropriateness of those persons selected to be raters.

- Use a clear report format. It must be easy for participants to decipher their feedback report. Graphic representation of data is helpful (e.g., bar charts and pie charts can effectively convey strengths, weaknesses, and comparisons).
- Convey relevance. Simply reading the report may not be adequate to motivate change because not all participants will be ready to change. Psychologists have found that readiness for change is a gradual process whereby individuals admit that change is necessary, develop the will and confidence to change, and finally commit to a specific behavioral action plan. A participant who has not yet become conscious of a need to change may be blind to the relevance of the feedback and its applicability. In such cases, there may be resistance to or discounting of the feedback. Tying the feedback to a participant's MBTI profile, for example, may help, but it may not be until a second opportunity arises to receive 360-degree feedback (perhaps 12 to 18 months later) that a participant begins to believe that the feedback is relevant.

## Feedback to Participants

Most providers of 360-degree feedback processes, including the Center for Creative Leadership, recommend consultative coaching for participants when they receive their feedback report. To assimilate the information, identify meaningful themes and patterns, and relate the feedback to their own work behavior, participants can be significantly aided by management consultants and coaches experienced with the 360-degree inventory being used. A coach can help the participant identify specific developmental activities and draft a plan based on the feedback.

### Development Plan

A written, detailed development plan helps the participant think through the actions required to change his or her behavior. Some 360-degree feedback products (e.g., Acumen Leadership Skills and Seven Habits Profile) provide suggestions for developmental activities.

Although participants often home in on what they consider negative feedback when they make choices for their development plan, positive behaviors (i.e., strengths) should also be reinforced. Further development of a strength may be more helpful to both the participant and the company than the improvement of a weakness.

Whatever is chosen, a step-by-step plan must be drafted and discussed with the participant's supervisor, with the supervisor acting in the key role of supporter, coach, and partner to ensure that the areas of development that the participant chooses are "in sync" with the strategic goals of the department and company. If the 360-degree feedback process is being used for performance appraisal purposes, the development plan takes on added weight for the participant's future with the organization.

### Follow-Up

The adage "What gets inspected gets respected" holds true for a 360-degree feedback development plan. Anecdotal evidence shows that those participants who check in periodically with their supervisors to discuss their progress during the period covered by their developmental plan have greater improvement on their next 360-degree feedback assessment than the participants who do not check in. This improvement comes from the following factors:

- Focus on the behavior to be changed. One participant in a 360-degree feedback program acknowledged, "I had my feelings hurt the first time, but I found myself using it throughout the year to guide me."
- The extra motivation of knowing one is accountable for change.
- The support and guidance of the supervisor.

## Accountability for Change

Although improved performance is the ultimate goal of a 360-degree feedback process, experts disagree about whether it is better to use this process for developmental or appraisal purposes. Experts who favor its use solely for developmental purposes (including experts at the Center for Creative Leadership) advocate that participation be voluntary and that the results be given only to the participant. This approach leaves change strictly up to the motivation of the participant. Proponents also believe that this approach it promotes the most nonbiased feedback. Because the feedback is not used for appraisal or for pay decisions, raters will be more candid and not as likely to shade the feedback to help (or harm) a boss or a colleague.

The experts who favor using 360-degree feedback for appraisal purposes believe that if the participant is free to disregard the feedback, which is often the case when it is used just for development, there will probably be little or no change. The report will probably sit on a shelf. These proponents believe that unless the feedback is available to the participant's supervisor and used either formally or informally as part of an appraisal process, there is no way to hold the participant accountable to the supervisor and the organization for improved performance. Some organizations have dealt with this controversy by giving a participant one or two "rounds" of developmental 360-degree feedback before using the feedback for appraisal. This approach gives the participant an opportunity to gain the perceptions of others, create a development plan based on the feedback, and start making behavioral changes.

A strategy to improve the likelihood of change is to repeat the process of assessment, feedback, and developmental planning in approximately 18 months. A period of less than 18 months is generally too short for the participant to identify developmental activities, create the plan, and have a development discussion with his or her supervisor. It also takes a while for the improved behavior to become refined and for others to notice the improvement.

Participants are often more convinced by the second feedback report than by the first. When similar patterns of information appear a second time, participants find it more difficult to discount the feedback or believe it is not relevant to them.

Ideally, the same individuals who were raters the first time are raters the second time. That situation rarely happens, though, because of staff changes. In spite of a few substitutions, patterns of behavior tend to hold true the second time, with the greatest improvements appearing in the areas that participants have targeted for particular effort.

In addition to following up with the participant, it is important to analyze the effectiveness of the 360-degree feedback instrument itself. Does it continue to be in alignment with the organization's strategic goals? Does it measure what is truly important for the individual's career success? Do participants report that they experience a benefit from the process? Is the benefit worth the time and money required to secure the feedback in this way?

A well-planned 360-degree feedback process has many benefits for participants and their organizations. As one feedback participant related, the process helped him "identify and face things I suspected and made me realize I can't keep sweeping them under the carpet. I realize how much more successful I and the company would be if I made some changes."

## References and Suggested Readings

Brown, S., & Cole, B. (1998). Does 360-degree feedback lead to change? *Management Development Forum, 1*(2), 41–52.

Coates, D. (1998). Breakthroughs in multisource feedback software. *Human Resource Professional, 11*(6), 7–11.

Huet-Cox, G. D., Nielson, T. M., & Sundstrom, E. (1999, May). Get the most from 360-degree feedback: Put it on the Internet. *HRMagazine,* 92–97.

Kaplan, R., & Palus, C. (1994). *Enhancing 360-degree feedback for senior executives.* Greensboro, NC: Center for Creative Leadership.

London, M., Smither, J., & Adsit, D. (1997). Accountability: The Achilles' heel of multisource feedback. *Group and Organization Management, 22*(2), 162–184.

Morical, K. (1999, April). A product review: 360 assessments. *Training and Development,* 43–47.

Nowack, K., Hartley, J., & Bradley, W. (1999, April). How to evaluate your 360 feedback efforts. *Training and Development,* 48–53.

Prochaska, J., DiClemente, C., & Norcross, J. (1992). In search of how people change: Applications to addictive behaviors. *American Psychologist, 47*(9), 1102–1114.

## Chapter 9

# Evaluating Team Performance

*James R. Jose*

O
ne of the demands imposed by the transition from high command and control to participative organizational cultures has been the requirement to change the methods used to evaluate work performance. Specifically, HR professionals have been challenged to change from exclusively evaluating people who perform in their individual capacities to evaluating people who perform as members of groups or teams. Team performance evaluation requires a shift of paradigms from single-rater processes to multirater processes and from an individual contributor focus to a more synergistic focus.

However, the shift does not require the abandonment of all of the definitive features of traditional evaluation models. For example, evaluating the effectiveness of teams requires performance expectations that are linked to business objectives and organizational values. Performance measures are essential, as are clear and easily understood rating systems. Individual development can continue to be at the core of the evaluation effort. Finally, consequences in the form of recognition and rewards (or lack thereof for nonachievement) should be an integral part of the evaluation process.

## The Challenge of Evaluating Teams

The evaluation of teams presents both raters and those being rated with special circumstances and opportunities. Teams are expected to have goals and objectives that they have, in large part, developed themselves. Typically, teams are intentionally composed of individuals with diverse backgrounds, experiences, longevity, and levels of influence. This diversity factor heightens the propensity for periodic value conflicts that must be managed by the team. This factor also creates an opportunity for the emergence of multiple and highly diverse options for goal achievement.

A wide range of interpersonal knowledge, skills, and abilities must be applied with more intensity in a team-based environment. For example, some knowledge about personality and decision-making types by team members and raters is desirable, as are highly developed collaborative and cooperative skills. The ability to participate constructively and to encourage other team members to do the same is necessary for teams to produce results. Producing results means that team members must master the giving and receiving of constructive feedback.

## Evaluation Methods

Both single-rater and multirater team evaluation processes are used in organizations today. The characteristics of the organizational culture usually determine which process is used. Specifically, defining characteristics include the extent to which teams are valued as a way of getting work done and whether they are encouraged to mature to a high performing level. The experience of the organization with the performance evaluation process and how the process is typically implemented in the organization are also important determinants. For example, if the evaluation process is typically used as a means of passing judgment on past work to the exclusion of developmental considerations, this bias will tend to carry over to team evaluations.

### Single-Rater Process Model

The single-rater process is the preference of organizations that create teams primarily to work on ad hoc, finite initiatives such reorganizing divisions, designing strategic plans, and developing workplace diversity programs. Those organizations typically have not had extensive experience with teamwork. They have performance appraisal processes that are supervisor driven, sometimes, although usually not, with input from other sources such as the employees themselves, peers, and clients. The organization's culture is characterized as hierarchical, high command-control, and possibly having some tentative experience with teams. Typically, teamwork is not highly valued as a way of getting work done.

The individual or group responsible for overseeing the work of the team is the rater, usually referred to as the sponsor or steering committee. Team members may be asked informally for their perspective on their own performance, but such feedback is not normally formalized as part of the evaluation.

Performance feedback may be provided to the team and to individual team members throughout the life of the team. Periodic progress checks usually take place at key milestones that were established when the team was formed. Formal performance evaluations of individual team members are completed in accordance with the company's performance appraisal timetable—usually, annually.

## Multirater Process Model

The multirater process is more appealing to organizations that have had successful experiences with teamwork and have moved beyond the traditional supervisor-driven performance evaluation process. These organizations would have had some experience with the 360-degree feedback process, and this process would have achieved a reasonable degree of acceptance within the employee group as a desirable and effective performance evaluation method. The culture is typically in the process of moving from hierarchical, high command-control to being more highly participative in nature, and the number of supervisory levels has been compressed. Teamwork would have a moderate to high level of acceptance as a way of getting work done.

Raters include the team itself, acting either collectively or individually, the steering committee or team leader to whom the team is responsible, and the representative of client groups and, possibly, other stakeholders as well. The team's self-evaluation and the input of all other participants in the evaluation process are considered formal parts of the evaluation.

Performance feedback to individuals and to the team as a whole is provided as an integral part of the team operation. Team members are comfortable in giving and receiving caring, constructive feedback as needed or as requested, or both, especially during team meetings. Formal progress checks take place at key milestones that were usually established when the team was formed. Formal performance evaluations are completed in accordance with the company's performance appraisal timetable.

## Evaluation Content

In both the single-rater and multirater processes, the team evaluation focuses on the performance expectations and desired results established in the team charter. The evaluation includes comments that reference the following areas:

- The effect of team activities on the business objectives and values of the company and any client groups
- The achievement of desired results (i.e., key deliverables) according to pre-established milestones
- The identification of team behavior trends such as adhering to operating

ground rules; giving and receiving caring, constructive feedback; and providing opportunities for team members to make individual contributions and to participate
- The identification of team strengths and group opportunities for change and development for the next performance period

## Conclusion

Experience reveals several guidelines that should be observed in the evaluation of team performance. First, the evaluation should be deliberate and have a purpose. Generally, three team evaluation purposes, which can be employed individually or in combination, predominate:

- To assess the extent to which the team is producing desired results and accomplishing its mission and objectives
- To determine how well the team is functioning as a participative decision-making organization
- To measure individual team member performance

Second, effective team evaluations have a self-evaluation component. The more mature the team, the greater the chances of the team knowing itself well and being willing to share that knowledge for its own development and that of the organization as a whole.

Third, evaluating individual as well as team performance is important. This evaluation is based on the assumption that team members are valued for the special gifts they bring to the mission, and, in turn, the team is valued for how well it elevates and integrates those gifts to produce the intended results.

## References and Suggested Readings

American Compensation Association. (1999). *Measuring team performance: A seven step guide to team success* (No. 47).

Chang, R. (1996). *Measuring organizational improvement impact.* Irvine, CA: Richard Chang Associates.

Chang, R. (1999). *Success through teamwork: A practical guide to interpersonal team dynamics.* San Francisco: Jossey-Bass.

Colenso, M. (2000). *Kaizen strategies for improving team performance.* Upper Saddle River, NJ: Financial Times/Prentice-Hall.

Dew, J. R. (1998). *Managing in a team environment.* Westport, CT: Greenwood.

Harrington-Mackin, D. (1994, March/April). Evaluating and rewarding team performance. *Compensation and Benefits Review, 26,* 67.

Henderson, D., & Green, F. (1997, January/February). Measuring self-managed work teams. *Journal for Quality and Participation, 20*(1), 52–57.

Hurley, S. (1998). Application of team-based 360° feedback systems. *Team Performance Management, (4)5,* 202–210.

Imperato, G. (1998, September). How Con-Way reviews teams. *Fast Company, 17,* 152.

Johns Hopkins University Staff. (2000). *Building a problem solving team.* Cincinnati, OH: South-Western College Publishing.

Jones, S. D. (2000). *Measuring team performance.* San Francisco: Jossey-Bass.

Margerison, C., & McCann, D. (2000). *Team management: Practical new approach.* Management Books 2000.

McAdams, J. L. (1996). *The reward plan advantage.* San Francisco: Jossey-Bass.

Moran, L., Musselwhite, E., Harrison, J., & Zenger, J. (1996). *Keeping teams on track: What to do when the going gets rough.* Chicago: Irwin Professional Publishing.

Nagler, B. (1998, January). Recasting employees into teams. *Workforce, 77*(1), 101–106.

Nash, S. S. (1999). *Turning team performance inside out: Team types and temperament for high-impact results.* Palo Alto, CA: Davies-Black Publishing.

O'Reilly, C. (2000). *Hidden value: How great companies achieve extraordinary results with ordinary people.* Cambridge, MA: Harvard Business School Press.

Parker, G. M. (1997). *Cross-functional teams tool kit.* San Francisco: Pfeiffer & Co.

Pokras, S. (2000). *Building high performance teams.* London: Kogan Page.

Rushmer, R. K. (1997). How do we measure the effectiveness of team building? Is it good enough? Team Management Systems—a case study. *Team Performance Management, 3*(4), 244–260.

Shonk, J. H. (1996). *Team-based organizations: Developing a successful team environment.* Chicago: Irwin Professional Publishing.

Stewart, G. L., Manz, C., & Sims, H. P. (1998). *Team work and group dynamics.* New York: John Wiley & Sons.

Sunoo, B. (2000, March). Around the world in HR ways. *Workforce, 79*(3), 54–58.

Valle, M., & Davis, K. (1999). Teams and performance appraisal: Using metrics to increase reliability and validity. *Team Performance Management, 8*(5), 238–244.

Zigon, J. (1998). *Performance measurement examples.* Media, PA: Zigon Performance Group.

Zigon, J. (1999). *How to measure team performance.* Media, PA: Zigon Performance Group.

## Chapter 10

# Assessing Employee Participation

*Heidi Connole and Maureen J. Fleming*

n today's competitive business environment, if there is one word that summarizes what should be the focus of human resource (HR) practitioners in the areas of employee participation and employee help programs, it is "collaboration." For the purpose of this discussion, collaboration is defined as both the process and the product of one person working with and in support of another. It means that HR practitioners need input and information from a wider variety of sources than those traditionally used when they engage in the decision-making process for the evaluation of employee participation and help programs.

To be successful, the concept of collaboration needs to be thoroughly integrated into the organization's strategy. The organization's culture must be collaborative (i.e., supportive of participation). The HR policies and practices must be the product of a collaborative process (i.e., based on information and input from a wide variety of sources). Finally, the assessment and evaluation of HR practices and policies must be in itself a collaborative process.

## How Much of a Good Thing Is Too Much?

It may be necessary to address the likely objections to the collaborative approach before one learns how to apply the concept of collaboration to the assessment of an employee participation or help program. Both scientific and anecdotal evidence establish the pros and cons of collaboration in general. For example, collaborative decisions are said to be more inclusive of the group as a whole, more representative, easier to support and sell to others, and closer to a "best case" solution to a dilemma. The trade-off is that collaboration is significantly more resource intensive, requiring more energy, more effort, more people, and, importantly, more time.

The real objections to using collaboration (especially in the process of assessing the effectiveness of HR practices or policies) are not likely to be found in a dispute over those pros and cons. The real objections are the legitimate, pragmatic concerns of HR practitioners who are responsible for decision making in the collaborative context. When evaluating the effectiveness of a given program, HR practitioners need to know how to avoid "information" overload. How does one screen information for its relevance to the program's evaluation? The answer lies in the application of strategic human resource management.

## Strategic Human Resource Management

Strategic human resource management (strategic HRM) is a relatively new but successful approach to evaluating HR practices and policies within an organization. The basic idea is to extend the assessment of the effectiveness of a given HR practice, policy or program to include an assessment of its strategic contribution. Although there are a variety of explanations of what constitutes a strategic contribution, it is generally agreed that strategic HRM requires a focus on the relationship between HR practices, policies, and programs and any of a variety of organizational outcomes of interest (Chadwick & Cappelli, 1999). Three commonly studied organizational outcomes follow (Chadwick & Cappelli, 1999):

• The effects of HR policies and programs on the financial performance of the firm
• The relationship between various HR decisions and the management of a firm's competitive environment
• The "fit" between the HR practices and the firm's strategy

HR practitioners can use those organizational outcomes as guidelines in the development and implementation of policy. Evidence supporting the use of a strategic HRM approach is found in a number of studies. For example, a recent analysis of 39 organizations found that changes in the organizations' culture, including changes in cooperation, innovation, and HR practices (e.g., reward and selection), have a positive influence on "the financial and operational performance of these organizations" (Varma, Beatty, Schneier, & Ulrich, 1999). Catlette and Hadden (1999) found that an organization's culture affects its ability to be competitive in attracting and retaining "good" employees. It is significant that the ideal culture was found to be collaborative. The ideal, collaborative culture communicates a common purpose and sense of direction, provides talented workers with meaningful work, and makes employees feel that they are competent, valued, and treated fairly.

Youden (1999) found that compensation, work satisfaction, relationships with managers and co-workers, career development, and job fit were key factors in reducing turnover in organizations. Cultures that facilitate the integration of these factors into their HR strategy create participative, nurturing, and collaborative environments.

Collectively, such studies show the successful application of strategic HRM although each study focuses on a different outcome of interest: firm performance, competitive environment management, and firm strategy–HR practice fit. When successfully applied, strategic HRM guides HR practitioners in their search for the type of information that is needed to evaluate the effectiveness of a practice or a policy. What makes strategic HRM a desirable companion approach to collaboration is its ability to focus the HR practitioner's attention on relevant information without restricting the process. The HR practitioner can still gather information and input from the widest variety of sources available but now has a way to categorize that information in terms of its usefulness in the program assessment and evaluation process.

## Application to Employee Participation and Assistance Programs

Collaboration is intuitively at the heart of any employee participation or assistance program. The spirit of such programs is found in the desire to work together toward a "best" outcome for all relevant parties—the proverbial "win-win" solution to managing human resources.

Employee participation programs can take a variety of forms, including (but not limited to) autonomous work groups, quality circles, participative work design projects, work rescheduling, participation-based compensation, and employee stock ownership plans (Cascio, 1991). The goal is to allow flexibility in the job design so that both the needs of the employee and the organization are met in an optimal way.

In the past, the novelty of such participation programs meant that the key question in assessing their effectiveness was to compare any of a number of relevant variables before the program's implementation and to look at those variables after a period of successful functioning for the program. Because the implementation of a participation program represented a new way of conducting the HR management process, the key question in evaluating the program was always Did change occur, and was it related to the implementation of a participation program? Answering this question depended on the use of a pretest-posttest design that compares measures taken before the implementation to measures obtained after the implementation is complete.

Today, in an era in which participation programs are more widespread, the evaluation of a given program is only related to change if it is a new implementation. More commonly, the question has become Are the participation programs currently in use contributing to the overall goals of strategic human resource management? This type of evaluation begins with a clear definition of "effectiveness" because the definition itself will play a key role in determining the best method for assessing a given program.

"Employee assistance programs" is the collective term given to a variety of services provided to employees in response to a host of personal problems. The programs include medical and psychological treatment for drug and alcohol abuse; marital, family, financial, and career counseling; and treatment for stress and emotional disorders. The rationale behind the implementation of such programs is to facilitate the well-being of employees who might otherwise become problems for the organization. Referral is made on both a self-initiated and supervisor-identified basis. Traditionally, the service is provided by an outside contractor so that the employee's confidentiality is ensured.

This situation creates a unique measurement problem for HR managers. The best information concerning actual use of the program could be obtained from the outside provider. However, under no circumstances should the quest for such information undermine the confidentiality promised to users. Generally, the only data available from such a source are aggregated data segmented by category of use (e.g., alcohol or financial counseling).

## Assessing the Effectiveness of HR Programs

The first step in assessing any type of HR program or policy is to define what is meant by "effectiveness." Managers can build meaningful definitions and, subsequently, evaluations of effectiveness from the framework suggested by Chadwick & Cappelli's (1999) organizational outcomes. These outcomes are incorporated in the following three-part question that can be asked of any participation or employee assistance program: (a) Does the program contribute to the financial performance of the firm, (b) does it contribute to the firm's ability to remain competitive in the market, and (c) is it consistent with the overall mission of the firm?

In some instances, the relationship between a given HR practice or policy and the organizational outcome of interest may be less direct. This situation is often the case with participation and employee assistance programs (EAPs), and in those instances, the appropriate measure of effectiveness may require evaluation of an intermediary step in the process. For example, the adoption of

EAPs may affect employee organizational commitment, which, in turn, may reduce the turnover rate and may affect the firm's bottom line.

Why is it important to connect participation and employee assistance programs to outcomes such as firm financial performance, competitiveness, or strategic congruence? To answer this question, the HR practitioner must tend to three relevant considerations. First, there is little agreement among researchers as to which HRM practices should be included in such studies (Becker & Gerhart, 1996; Chadwick & Cappelli, 1999; Wright & Sherman, 1999). However, it does seem clear that HRM practices that are not consistent with the firm's strategy as a whole have an adverse effect on the firm's overall organizational performance. Second, some researchers have suggested that HR practices are often adopted as a means of seeking legitimacy from social and political institutions rather than as the result of a strategic choice initiative (Spell & Blum, 1996). Succumbing to pressures for conformity is contradictory to the idea of strategic HRM. Third, the process of tying HR practices to strategy has identified the need for both flexibility and fit in HRM for an employer to remain competitive, particularly in volatile environments (Milliman, Von Glinow, & Nathan, 1991).

## Appropriate Measurement Techniques

Once a definition of effectiveness has been established, the second step in the assessment of HR programs is to determine which methodology will be most appropriate for collecting and analyzing relevant data. Quantitative methods are usually used to assess job performance because such data can be easily analyzed with quantitative techniques (e.g., mean, mode, and median performance ratings) or more advanced statistical techniques made available by software packages (such as SPSS and SAS). Some examples of the types of variables that lend themselves to such analysis are: turnover, absenteeism, and accident rates; sales performance or production volume; or scores on objective assessments of knowledge, skills, or attributes. If an organization has implemented an employee stock ownership program, for example, a quantitative measurement of employee turnover or absenteeism rates might contribute to understanding the program's effectiveness, thereby enhancing organizational commitment.

Qualitative methods are generally used to assess perceptual or attitudinal criteria. The most common approach is the written survey questionnaire. A short Likert-style scale that asks questions about satisfaction with and the importance of various aspects of the worker participation or employee assistance program can be useful and easily converted to data that can be analyzed with similar quantitative techniques.

Other qualitative methods yield responses that are not as easily coded for analysis or aggregated to generalize across individuals. Such methods include in-depth interviews, observation of individuals in their actual work environments, and analysis of textual documents (e.g., internal memos, e-mail communications) that provide a richer, "thicker" description of actual interactions and benefits of the programs of interest. Historically, qualitative methods have often been used for the initial investigation of a question as a way of exploring it in order to design Likert-style scales or to identify appropriate quantitative measures for analysis.

In the example using EAP and participation programs to assess effectiveness of HR programs, HR managers could assess the relationship between participation and employee assistance programs and the level of organizational commitment of employees by conducting in-depth interviews of individuals who are at various stages of their tenure with the company. The interviews will provide a rich and detailed understanding of a program's benefits and value from the employee's perspective. Next, the manager may develop a Likert-style scale that asks employees to rate their level of satisfaction with the programs on the basis of the information gleaned from the analysis of the in-depth interviews.

In a triangulation of methods approach that is advocated by many researchers, HR managers compare, contrast, or combine data from both quantitative and qualitative methods as a means of increasing their confidence in the outcome data (Zamanou & Glaser, 1994). In the example above, with this approach, the HR manager would collect both quantitative (e.g., absenteeism and turnover rates) and qualitative data (e.g., interview or survey data) as a means of assessing the effectiveness of a given program or its effect on an outcome variable of interest (here, organizational commitment). The integration of findings from methodologies strengthens the conclusions drawn by managers.

Although the example provided has focused on employee participation programs, quantitative and qualitative methods can also be used effectively in the assessment of EAPs. In that case, a triangulation approach may be necessary because the issue of employee confidentiality makes it difficult to gather that data.

Furthermore, the assessment of the employee assistance program's strategic plan is complicated by the fact that the ideal situation is one in which most employees have very little need or use for the service. In this sense, "effectiveness" may best be defined in terms of employee awareness of the availability of the service, attractiveness of the firm's offering as an employment benefit, and employee confidence in and general satisfaction with the program.

From the strategic HRM perspective, the ultimate goal of the program evaluation process is to examine a given program's strategic contribution. To determine the strategic contribution, one examines the relationship between the measure of the assessment of the program and the measure of one or more of the organizational outcomes of interest (Chadwick & Cappelli, 1999) previously discussed.

As shown above, some variables lend themselves more readily to either quantitative or qualitative measures. Firm performance is traditionally measured quantitatively, while competitiveness and strategic congruence are perhaps better measured by qualitative methods or a combination of quantitative and qualitative measures.

If HR managers wanted to evaluate the organization's EAP from a strategic HRM approach, they would take the following steps. First, they would define "program effectiveness." In keeping with the example above, "effectiveness" might be defined as employee awareness of the EAP. Second, the managers would measure employee awareness. In this case, a survey of a sample of the organization's employees would provide the information. Third, the managers would examine the relationship between employee awareness of the program (perhaps as determined by a survey) and the firm's financial performance, competitiveness, and strategic congruence. The program would be said to make a strategic contribution when there was a detectable relationship between an increase in awareness of the program and any of the following:

- A lower turnover rate that affects the firm's operating costs and subsequently the firm's net profit (i.e., financial performance)
- An increased ability of the firm to fill available positions with quality applicants (i.e., competitiveness)
- The achievement of a strategic goal to lower accident or product defect rates caused by employee error (i.e., strategic congruence)

The scenario above is just a single example of how these concepts might be applied. A variety of alternative measures could be used to define "success" in terms of financial performance, competitiveness, or strategic congruence.

## Conclusion

Cabrera and Bonache suggest that a strategic culture is one in which the HR practices are carefully planned to promote the "behavioral norms necessary for achieving the organization's strategy" (1999). Those authors further state that selection must be deliberate in order to choose candidates whose own values are consistent with the organization's cultural norms.

As managers seek to apply the advice, there is a growing need for including in the evaluation of employee participation and assistance programs an assessment of how these programs make a strategic contribution to the organization. Greengard (1999) suggests that HR managers have grown quite adept at using surveys to make related assessments but that this type of study is often inadequate, failing to take into account the dynamic nature of what is being assessed. Bacon (1999) writes that "it is timely to reconsider HRM from the perspective of the shop/office floor worker." Such a perspective requires a more time-consuming, comprehensive, and in-depth inquiry into the effectiveness of participation and employee assistance programs. In short, what is advocated is collaboration—an organizational culture that supports collaboration: HR programs, policies, and practices that are a product of collaboration; and assessment techniques and measures that involve a collaborative process.

## References and Suggested Readings

Bacon, N. (1999). The realities of human resource management? *Human Relations, 52*(9), 1179.

Becker, B., & Gerhart, B. (1996). The impact of human resources management on organizational performance: Progress and prospects. *Academy of Management Journal, 39,* 779–801.

Cabrera, E. F., & Bonache, J. (1999). An expert HR system for aligning organizational culture and strategy. *Human Resource Planning, 22*(1), 51.

Cascio, W. F. (1991). *Applied psychology in personnel management.* Englewood Cliffs, NJ: Prentice-Hall.

Catlette, B., & Hadden, R. (1999). Are your cows content? *Workforce, 78*(4), 61.

Chadwick, C., & Cappelli, P. (1999). Alternatives to generic strategy typologies in strategic human resource management. In P. Wright et al. (Eds.), *Research in personnel and human resources management: Suppl. 4. Strategic human resources management in the 21st century* (pp. 11–29). Greenwich, CT: JAI Press.

Greengard, S. (1999). Surveying the HR landscape. *Workforce, 78*(8), 100.

Milliman, J., Von Glinow, M. A., & Nathan, M. (1991). Organizational life cycles and strategic international human resource management in multinational companies: Implications for congruence theory. *Academy of Management Review, 16,* 318–339.

Spell, C. S., & Blum, T. C. (1996 August). *Pre-employment drug testing: Weapon in the war on drugs or response to the institutional environment?* Paper presented at the meeting of the Academy of Management, Cincinnati, OH.

Varma, A., Beatty, R. W., Schneier, C. E., & Ulrich, D. (1999). High performance work systems: Exciting discovery or passing fad? *Human Resource Planning, 22*(1), 26.

Wright, P. M., & Sherman, W. S. (1999). Failing to find fit in strategic human resource management: Theoretical and empirical problems. In P. Wright et al. (Eds.), *Research in personnel and human resources management: Suppl. 4. Strategic human resources management in the 21st century* (pp. 53–74). Greenwich, CT: JAI Press.

Youden, P. (1999). Job satisfaction key to building team. *Triangle Business Journal, 14*(45), 19.

Zamanou, S., & Glaser, S. R. (1994). Moving toward participation and involvement. *Group and Organization Management, 19*(4), 475–502.

# Chapter 11

# Evaluating Training Effectiveness

## *Jonathan S. Monat*

The essential model for evaluating organizational training and development programs has been a standard framework in the training and development (T&D) literature since it was first published in 1967. The model requires that T&D programs be evaluated in four phases: (a) trainee reaction, (b) learning during training, (c) transfer of training, and (d) results of training. In practice, more attention is given to the first category than to the other three. In the competitive environment, the reality is that the latter three categories of evaluation are more important to an organization's bottom line and should be an integral part of the T&D program.

Organizations provide training to their members for many reasons. As businesses move into the information age, the need for continuous improvement will increase the demand for T&D in organizations. As organizations grow more dependent on T&D, evaluation of those programs becomes a critical management tool. For evaluation to be effective, it must be planned in advance to assure that what is being evaluated is consistent with the objectives of the T&D program and the organization. The evaluator must define the desired terminal behaviors and organizational outcomes along with measures of these behaviors and outcomes.

Evaluation is a process or planned set of activities that compares actual results against specified objectives and established criteria. Consideration must be given to criterion sampling across all job dimensions, situations, and behavioral and organizational outcomes to assure a complete set of data. Because some effects of T&D are not immediately apparent or measurable for extended periods, it is critical to conduct evaluations over a sufficient time period with a focus on terminal behaviors, results, cost/benefits, and return on investment (ROI).

## Requirements for Evaluation Criteria

A criterion is a measure of desired outcomes, results, or performance. A good criterion (or set of criteria) for evaluation must be reliable, providing consistent information when used at different times and by different trainers or supervisors. Often overlooked while the focus is on statistical tests of reliability are the requirements that a criterion must be relevant, uncontaminated, not deficient, acceptable, and practical. "Relevant" means that measures of training outcomes and what is learned in training must be related. At the end of a training program, the relevant criteria for evaluation are the same as the criteria used to measure on-the-job performance.

Criterion contamination occurs when capabilities that are not part of the training program are measured or when external conditions affect evaluation. Managers need to be trained so that trainees are measured objectively on the capabilities learned in the training program and managers are not influenced by managerial bias or political necessity. External conditions refer to factors such as equipment, software, time constraints, or other working conditions that may be different from the conditions under which training took place. If the trainee is faced with factors different from those found in the training environment, it will be difficult to measure the extent to which learned skills transfer to the job. In reality, conditions in training and on the job are rarely identical. The extent to which conditions vary can contaminate measurements.

Trainees and trainers both must accept a criterion measure as relevant or it will be ignored by one or the other. Trainees must see the training, sometimes called "face validity," as relevant to their work and improved performance. Criteria should be practical, and observing and measuring behaviors should not be too costly in time, money, and administration.

## Validity of the Criteria

Once its reliability has been established, a good criterion must also have validity. In other words, Did T&D cause changes in behavior, or can the results be explained by some other factor? Also, Does training provide the planned outcomes at an acceptable cost? The most comprehensive evaluation strategies will combine elements of experimental and statistical design with managerial decision models based on contribution to profit, ROI, and cost-effectiveness. Experimental and statistical designs, which measure the validity of the training, in effect ask Did training achieve intended objectives? If so, was the training cost-effective? The latter question cannot be answered without answering the first question.

Experimental and statistical analyses determine whether the changes in performance were the direct result of the training or arose from other factors such as maturation, the effect of contemporaneous events, history, or pretesting and trainee selection (i.e., Hawthorne) effects. The consideration of maturation is especially important when planning training programs that take a long time to complete—especially if a company has problems with retention. Selecting trainees for specific characteristics may affect internal validity; that consideration is especially important in larger organizations. A narrow set of characteristics may not give a true picture of the validity of training and generalizing the results across the whole organization may not be possible. In one large county government training program involving 5,000 managers, a specific requirement for each training group of 25 is that the members of the group be drawn from across many departments. This practice has the advantage of increasing relevance, acceptability, and ability to generalize.

A number of experimental designs that use different numbers of training and control groups are available for the HR practitioner. Sources listed at the end of this chapter contain useful discussions of these designs. A careful reading will help the practitioner select the design that satisfies the needs; the resources (i.e., time, staff, and money); the requirements for the type of training; and the number and frequency of trainees.

## Profitability and Cost

Although the validity of a T&D program is of most interest to the trainer, management poses the most significant evaluation: Does the T&D program achieve its objectives at a reasonable cost? A cost-effectiveness (i.e., cost-benefit) model is the primary strategy to follow. Following such a model is advantageous because the evaluation is couched directly in managerial terms, thereby making it more acceptable to top management.

Results of training may be measured by profitability and cost with what is generally characterized as accounting data. Accounting data are especially useful in cost-effectiveness analysis and calculating the ROI from training. Quality control measures can provide direct and indirect insight on the behavioral outcomes of T&D. Productivity data provide another set of measures for results of training and can show the link between training and improved profitability. Cost-benefit analysis measures the effectiveness of one or more T&D programs as well as outcome effectiveness.

## Behavioral and Learning Criteria

Behavioral and quantitative criteria may be used at different learning stages during training and after periodic posttraining performance evaluations to demonstrate the effect of training over different time periods. Accounting and production data are especially useful at the results phase. At the learning and behavior levels, criteria are skill based, and the performance bar increases as proficiency increases. It is important that the same measurement techniques be used throughout the learning phase—from assessment to postlearning.

Because a well-planned T&D program is assembled in modules or building blocks based on job descriptions and component tasks, identifying the appropriate behavioral and learning criteria should flow directly from each module or block. Standards of performance become more stringent. As the building blocks are assembled into more complex modules, the ability of the learner to perform increasingly complex tasks is measured. Ultimately, the standards to be met are at the level of a fully trained and proficient jobholder.

In the evaluation of a corporation's physical fitness program, one trainer developed a set of measures for several time frames. Short-term criteria included behavioral and reaction measures. Long-term measures were cost based, emphasizing productivity factors, time and salary lost to illness, use of medical plans, and years of service. Personnel measures such as absenteeism and accident rates were used, along with attitude measures such as cooperation, adherence to safety practices, tolerance for diversity and satisfaction. Analysis of these types of data can provide insight into the degree to which training has achieved managerial goals and training objectives.

To answer questions about cost-effectiveness, the trainer must first develop a training budget. All costs associated with planning, implementing, and evaluating the training program should be identified. Fixed and variable costs, development costs, and the costs of training managers and supervisors as evaluators should be considered.

## Identifying Costs

All costs are either fixed or variable. Fixed costs are those costs that would be incurred whether or not the T&D program were implemented. Variable costs are those costs that are incurred only if the T&D program is carried out. Variable costs include direct costs of development and implementation of the T&D program, trainee participation, training of managers and supervisors, materials, food, and travel. Compensation costs should include the costs of benefits and any premium pay. The costs of training the trainers and the evaluators, as well as the costs of the evaluation process, should be calculated.

Blanchard and Thacker (1999) suggest that the question Is training worth the effort? can be answered using three types of analysis: cost-benefit, cost-effectiveness, and utility. Cost-benefit analysis compares the cost of training to the nonmonetary benefits. For example, the costs of a customer service training program could be compared with the level of service after training, as reported by customers. The critical step is to carefully define the anticipated benefits in observable and measurable terms.

Cost-effectiveness more directly compares the monetary costs of training with the financial benefits that flow from training. Cessna Flight Schools compared the fixed, variable, and total costs of training private pilots with its integrated, structured approach comprising text, video, class, and flying against the unstructured approach of community college ground school attendance followed by flight lessons after completion of ground school. Although students soloed after an average of 15 hours in the Cessna program as compared to about 10 hours in the unstructured program, Cessna students completed their private pilot license in about 55 hours as compared to 70 hours for students in the unstructured program. The cost savings to the students were well over a thousand dollars.

Utility analysis studies all the ways that a trainee's improved job performance will financially benefit the company and includes estimates of how long the benefits of training will last. The concept is that if the employees who are trained "are, on the average, better performers, and better performers are worth more in dollar terms, utility analysis permits the estimation of that increased worth" (Blanchard & Thacker, 1999). Blanchard and Thacker provided an example of financial benefits accruing from grievance training. Their excellent analysis can be widely applied to most types of managerial and behavioral training.

Which analysis to use depends both on the cost in dollars and time of conducting the analysis and on who needs to know what information. Reaction and learning data may be most important to trainers and not important to management. These data, often called "feel good" measures, are used primarily to assess learning and behavior change during training and transfer to the job. Trainees and training personnel want to know that trainees felt the training was worth their time away from their jobs and that the training had a degree of validity.

*Figure 11-1*_____

## Industrial Training Cost-Effectiveness Model

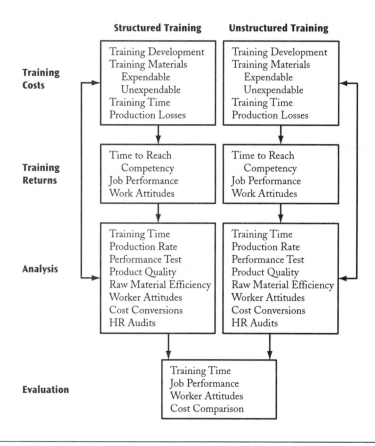

| | Structured Training | Unstructured Training |
|---|---|---|
| **Training Costs** | Training Development<br>Training Materials<br>  Expendable<br>  Unexpendable<br>Training Time<br>Production Losses | Training Development<br>Training Materials<br>  Expendable<br>  Unexpendable<br>Training Time<br>Production Losses |
| **Training Returns** | Time to Reach<br>  Competency<br>Job Performance<br>Work Attitudes | Time to Reach<br>  Competency<br>Job Performance<br>Work Attitudes |
| **Analysis** | Training Time<br>Production Rate<br>Performance Test<br>Product Quality<br>Raw Material Efficiency<br>Worker Attitudes<br>Cost Conversions<br>HR Audits | Training Time<br>Production Rate<br>Performance Test<br>Product Quality<br>Raw Material Efficiency<br>Worker Attitudes<br>Cost Conversions<br>HR Audits |
| **Evaluation** | Training Time<br>Job Performance<br>Worker Attitudes<br>Cost Comparison | |

## Outcome Data

Outcome data based on the results of performance are very important to management, but trainers often fail to provide this form of evaluation. The information must be worth the cost of collecting it. For example, an airline may be focused more on behavioral and learning outcomes of flight crew training than on cost savings or cost-benefits. Evaluation of the cost of different training technology would be relevant rather than evaluation of the need to conduct training, a given legal requirement. Figure 11–1 shows how one can integrate different forms of evaluation into a cost-effectiveness model. A detailed discussion of this approach may be found in Cullen (1978).

## Conclusion

The evaluation of training programs is complex. The needs of the organization dictate the types of evaluation employed and even the extent to which evaluation takes place. The benefits that a company receives from training must be weighed against all the costs of providing that training in this context. The extent of the evaluation process that is developed and the complexity of the evaluation models are based on intelligent analysis of the need to know. Seemingly hard-to-measure variables are in fact relatively easy to measure if thought and attention are given to evaluation as part of the development phase of any training program.

## References and Suggested Readings

Blanchard, P. N., & Thacker, J. W. *Effective training: Systems, strategies, and practices.* Englewood Cliffs, NJ: Prentice-Hall.

Coltrin, S. A. (1990). Training Programs. In F. J. Ofsanko & N. K. Napier (Eds.), *Effective human resource measurement techniques.* SHRM Foundation.

Cullen, J. G., et. al. (1978, January). Cost effectiveness: A model for assessing the training investment. *Training and Development Journal,* 1–4.

Donaldson, L., & Scannell, E. E. (1995). *Human resource development: The new trainer's guide.* Old Tappan, NJ: Addison Wesley.

Kirkpatrick, D. L. (Ed.) (1967). *Evaluating training programs* (pp. 1–17). Madison, WI: ASTD.

Mathis, R., & Jackson, J. (1999). *Human resource management* (9th Ed.). Cincinnati, OH: Southwestern/ITP.

Noe, R. A. (1999). *Employee training and development.* New York: Irwin McGraw-Hill.

# Chapter 12

# Cost Accounting Concepts in HRM

*Eric Anton Kreuter*

**H**uman resource (HR) managers are usually excellent at studying ways to make the workplace better for employees. Company-oriented managers also contribute to the bottom line of their employers through their consideration of the cost of HR-related programs and their relative effectiveness. Such profit-motivated HR managers try to anticipate the future impact on corporate profits that their proposed HR programs will likely have. In examining the design and implementation of effective HR measurement techniques, an HR practitioner must consider certain cost analyses. McDonald and Smith maintain that "historically, the HR function has defied quantification or measurement, which has left HR professionals ill-prepared to demonstrate that human resources are a form of capital, not solely a line entry of expense" (1995, p. 59). The authors, in describing a recent study by Hewitt Associates that analyzes data from 437 large companies, conclude that "managing human resources provides a payoff in bottom-line financial performance" (p. 59). The study further notes that performance management is key to improving financial results of troubled companies. Therefore, evidence suggests that even for an entity in financial trouble, resources expended to assess performance yield positive financial results.

The benefits to a company in having a quality performance management program are extensive. In the area of performance appraisals, it is best to look at results-based leadership. Results-based leadership performance appraisal measures the connection between the attributes of leadership and results. "Results-based leadership connects tightly to performance appraisals. The standard set for results-based leaders should focus on both the results, or ends, and the attributes, or means, needed to achieve them" (Ulrich, Zenger, & Smallwood, 1999, pp. 208–209). Through the establishment of goals and objectives, managers and leaders can set benchmarks. Costs involved with setting up a program, as well as the cost of administration, will be more than made up through increased effort and focus on the part of the managers and leaders. The objective is to motivate the team to be committed to the goals of the organization and to shape their activities to those goals.

HR managers need to develop a thorough understanding of business. The main objective of any manager is to maximize shareholder wealth while coinciding with corporate strategic planning. Some plans will be oriented toward short-term goals and others toward long-term goals.

## Cost-Benefit Analysis

The application of basic cost accounting principles to HR management is necessary and comparatively easy. The best way to start is to prepare a detailed cost-benefit analysis to measure the relative success of a given course of action. For example, if the cost of leasing a vehicle is less than the cost associated with ownership, leasing would be the sensible choice. It is helpful to view expenses associated with new programs as investments. This approach provides a clearer picture of the return on that investment or its benefit. The simple approach to cost determination is to prepare a schedule of all actual or possible categories of expenses or projected benefits. Then the relevant cost in dollars associated with each expense or benefit can be calculated. The example in the box on the following page illustrates the use of this technique.

Not all costs and benefits will be easy to measure. Mercer (1989, p. 15) maintains the following view: "Obviously, some [costs and benefits] are easier to measure than others are. Nonetheless, human resource managers must take it upon themselves to calculate all the possible monies involved in any human resources solutions to business problems. In this way everyone possesses a measure of how effective the human resources endeavors have been."

Mercer further recommends conservatism in cost accounting. All organized bodies of accounting and management would concur that it is best to present analyses realistically.

## Measuring the Economic Consequences of Corporate Restructuring

Corporate restructurings (resulting in terminations or "early-outs") have a significant effect on the cost analysis functions of managing human resources. "Although the administration of corporate early-outs is done by human resource managers, few understand the economic rationale behind the apparent obses-

**Problem:** Overtime pay is exceeding the budgeted amount.

**New Program (i.e., solution):** Hire an additional worker; eliminate overtime.

**Step 1:** Determine the relevant costs associated with the new program.

| | |
|---|---|
| Base compensation | $ 20,000 |
| Fringe benefits (25% of base compensation) | 5,000 |
| Training | 2,000 |
| Recruitment | 3,000 |
| Other | 1,000 |
| Total relevant costs | $ 31,000 |

**Step 2:** Project the benefit.

| | |
|---|---|
| Reduced overtime hours per year | 1,800 |
| Total overtime cost per hour | $ 19 |
| Total reduced overtime cost per year | $ 42,750 |
| (1,800 × $19) × 125% | |

**Step 3:** Calculate the savings.

| | |
|---|---|
| Total reduced overtime costs | $ 42,750 |
| Total relevant costs of the new program | (31,000) |
| Annual savings | $ 11,750 |

**Conclusion:** Hiring an additional worker and eliminating overtime will generate an annual savings of $11,750. Therefore, the benefit is greater than the cost, and the new program should be adopted.

sion that America's CEOs have with restructuring" (Berra & Whitford, 1995, p. 96). An interesting phenomenon is that stock prices often go up following an announcement of a planned restructuring. Shareholders feel optimistic that the long-range benefits of such actions will surpass the short-term costs. This thinking is consistent with the investment mentality that share prices should be a multiple of forward earnings. Therefore, if shareholders see positive future earnings growth, they will trade up the stock price regardless of the effect of the restructuring on current period earnings.

If managed properly, a workforce reduction will not result in decreased revenues. This revenue-neutral status is because of expected increases in worker productivity. The savings per worker can be calculated by taking into consideration the worker's base salary and adding fringe benefit costs. Then, applicable corporate tax deductions are subtracted. It is important to factor in an estimated inflation percentage. By decreasing costs, the company will decrease its need for capital. Such a situation dramatically affects the company's cost of operating. The following example illustrates this concept:

---

## Effect of a Workforce Reduction on Profitability

**Action:** Reduction in workforce by 5%

| | |
|---|---|
| Total number of terminated workers | 10 |
| Average base compensation | $ 35,000 |
| Fringe benefit factor | 25% |
| Other costs per worker | $ 3,000 |
| Applicable combined tax rate | 50% |

**Total savings calculated as follows:**

| | |
|---|---|
| Reduced compensation | $350,000 |
| Reduced fringe benefits | 87,500 |
| Reduced other costs | 30,000 |
| Total reduced costs | $467,500 |

**Capital costs:**

| | |
|---|---|
| Reduced capital costs | $ 37,400 |
| (8% of total reduced costs) | |
| Reduced combined costs | 504,900 |
| Less reduced tax benefit | (252,450)* |
| Net benefit | $252,450 |

*As a result of reduced cost, tax deductions will also decrease, yielding net savings of $252,450.

---

Offsetting the savings will be the exit compensation package, which is usually paid as a lump sum of salary and benefits. The after-tax cost can be calculated resulting in a current cost matched to the after-tax present value of an early-out restructuring. Therefore, each restructuring can be evaluated on the basis of its projected effect on the net present value (NPV) of the company's equity. The NPV measures the expected change in total stockholder wealth.

Within the cost analysis, HR managers and the corporate officers need to consider the potential negative effect of a restructuring on employee morale. Berra and Whitford maintain that "the early-out program could potentially decrease revenues or at least slow their growth significantly" (1995, p. 98). Some restructurings have a negative effect caused by expense reductions resulting in harm to the company's long-term viability. That result is due to decreased resource availability and lower employee morale.

## The Cost of Performance Appraisal Systems

Companies have been spending large sums of money to develop performance appraisal systems, many of which are later abandoned largely because of dissatisfaction with the systems. Pratt & Whitney, for example, "the jet engine division of United Technologies, made significant changes in its appraisal system in three consecutive years only to abandon the system for a completely different approach the very next year" (Bernadin, Kane, Ross, Spina, & Johnson, 1995, p. 463). Opponents of formal appraisal systems argue that fluctuation in performance is a function of system characteristics rather than individual characteristics. "Reengineering of operational processes to create a customer-focused organization suggests an accompanying reengineering of performance appraisal systems" (Bernadin et al., 1995, p. 464).

### Tailoring the Design

For a pay-for-performance compensation system to work effectively, performance measurement is required. The design of an effective appraisal is a challenge to organizations. "The details of the plan should be reviewed in order to design an appraisal system consistent with the overall goals of the organization and the environment in which the organization exists" (Bernadin et al., 1995, p. 468). A study by the National Research Council concluded that "the search for a high degree of precision in measurement does not appear to be economically viable in most applied settings; many believe that there is little to be gained from such a level of precision" (Bernadin et al., 1995, pp. 468–469).

### Using Automation to Decrease Costs

Automation has enabled companies to enter performance appraisal ratings, thus streamlining the data-gathering process. The advantages of this option include lower costs and easy integration of results into the computerized central personnel record system. For example, data can be entered in one location and transmitted electronically worldwide. With the increased capabilities of Internet use, recording results should be even easier. The use of computers eliminates clerical functions, paper records, and files. Computer use needs to be analyzed in terms of cost, including an assessment of the availability of computer terminals.

## Outsourcing

Outsourcing has become a popular management tool for controlling varying workloads and reducing payroll costs. In 1994, a survey of 79 companies by The Conference Board indicated that 85% were using or planning to use outside firms to handle some of the work of their HR departments. The most frequently outsourced HR functions, according to the survey, were administration of 401(k) plans or other retirement plans, employee assistance programs, wellness or fitness programs, relocation services, and other benefits (The Conference Board, 1994).

As employers look closely at the bottom-line contribution of the HR department, those functions that require special expertise or have little value-added benefit to the company will continue to be outsourced to specialists and vendors. Outsourcing can benefit a company's HR professionals by freeing them to focus on their most important tasks and by streamlining administrative tasks. For example, termination of the internal information systems personnel and simultaneous contracting of an outside service company to handle these functions will result in tangible benefits. Such benefits include greater depth of knowledge and skill and likely reduced total cost. Costs associated with employee benefits, recruitment, and time off will not be incurred.

## Variable Training Costs

Costs are typically categorized as either fixed or variable with some semivariable costs. The main determinant is the relationship between the amount of the specific cost and its relation to changes in revenue. We can look at rent expense as an example of a fixed cost, payroll as an example of variable cost, and power as a semivariable cost (e.g., factory power cost would increase if a second shift were commenced). Training cost should be viewed as variable. In this model, departments and personnel must earn the right to training by linking the concept of value to the product or the process to the training. This expectation is more appropriate in today's changing business environment and will prevent a company from offering the same programs each year.

> Training that runs like a business, in contrast, requires no such corporate subsidy. It operates as a variable cost, one that customers incur only at their own initiative. We believe there are inherent efficiencies in this pay-for-use approach to funding T & D [training and development], just as history has shown that there are inherent efficiencies in free-market economies (Adelsberg & Trolley, 1999, p. 36).

## References and Suggested Readings

Adelsberg, D. V., & Trolley, E. A., (1999). *Running training like a business.* San Francisco: Berrett-Koehler.

Bernadin, H. J. , Kane, J. S., Ross, S., Spina, J. D., & Johnson, D. L. (1995). Performance appraisal, design, development, and implementation. In G. R. Ferris, S. D. Rosen, & D. T. Barnum (Eds.), *Handbook of human resource management* (pp. 463–489). Cambridge, MA: Blackwell.

Berra, R. L., & Whitford, D. T. (1995). Analytical financial tools and human resource management. In G. R. Ferris, S. D. Rosen, & D. T. Barnum (Eds.), *Handbook of human resource management* (pp.83–98). Cambridge, MA: Blackwell.

The Conference Board. (1994). *HR executive review: Outsourcing HR services.* New York: Helen Axel.

McDonald, D., & Smith, A. (1995). A proven connection: Performance management, compensation and business results. In E. L. Gubman (Ed.), *Compensation and benefits review* (p. 59). New York: AMACOM (American Management Association).

Mercer, M. (1989). *Turning your human resources department into a profit center.* New York: AMACOM.

Syrett, M. (1987). New patterns of work. In S. Harper (Ed.), *Personnel management handbook* (pp. 121–135). London: Gower Publishing.

Ulrich, D., Zenger, J., & Smallwood, N. (1999). *Results-based leadership*. Boston: Harvard Business School Press.

# Chapter 13

# Shared Services

## Sharafat Khan and David Parent

**T**oday's corporate executives face a wider array of challenges than ever before. These challenges mirror the pressures of the global economy. Simultaneously, firms must maximize shareholder value, achieve growth targets, enhance operational flexibility, improve customer service, integrate suppliers and vendors, retain and develop technical and managerial leaders, and overcome a myriad of other challenges. In addressing these challenges, corporate leaders must find ways for their organizations to focus on the activities that truly add value to their business. Analyzing internal activities from this perspective prompts corporations to increasingly examine a critical question: How do we best organize critical business support activities in a manner that maximizes their value-added and directly contributes to achieving business objectives—but does so in an efficient, streamlined, and cost-effective manner?

Over the last decade, much has been written about the need for human resources (HR) functions to transform or re-invent themselves. Historically, HR organizations have been seen as personnel departments, administrators, and rule makers. However, to the function and the organization that HR departments belong to, this simplistic view of HR is no longer acceptable. Instead, HR practitioners must now be strategic business partners within their organizations, providing value-added programs, processes, activities, and services in a cost-effective manner. Toward this end, corporations have sought new and different ways to organize and deploy their HR budgets and staffs. In the 1980s, organizations began to reengineer their HR functions. Today, the focus has moved from reengineering to shared services. Improved human resource information systems (HRIS), enterprise-wide systems, and web-enabled technologies have served as catalysts for efforts to improve services while reducing costs. For example, 77% of respondents in a Deloitte & Touche/Lawson Software survey indicated that they were then undertaking or considering undertaking a project to improve or redesign HR-related processing. The focus of such efforts has been to ensure that HR meets the needs of the business while improving the returns on HR function investments.

Although shared services have been used more readily in redeploying finance and information technology functions in many companies, HR is seen as the next domain ready for shared services organization. The shared services concept has become popular with HR organizations because it offers the function a way to respond to several macrobusiness trends through one highly effective mechanism. HR organizations, like the corporations to which they belong, are grappling with challenges such as the following:

- Pressure to reduce budgets and expenditures
- Need to maximize productivity and to minimize headcounts by leveraging technology
- Demands for improved customer service, responsiveness, and focus

At the same time, HR functions are expected to address unique "human capital" issues such as

- Attracting and retaining a highly skilled workforce in a tight labor market
- Integrating and coordinating a global workforce
- Facilitating the organizational and cultural integration associated with mergers, acquisitions, and alliances
- Managing a "virtual" workforce and work environment
- Creating, maintaining, and distributing knowledge throughout the organization
- Leading efforts to foster and leverage a diverse workforce and work environment
- Building leadership talents in the current and future generations of organizational leaders

Many organizations are realizing that HR has a much greater role to play in ensuring corporate success. As many firms and industries have realized, human capital is the next competitive battlefield; the days of viewing HR as purely an administrative function are over.

## HR's Changing Image

For HR to step up and meet the challenges of its new role, it must change not only its image but also the way it has operated historically. Traditionally, HR

*Figure 13-1*

# Human Resources Models

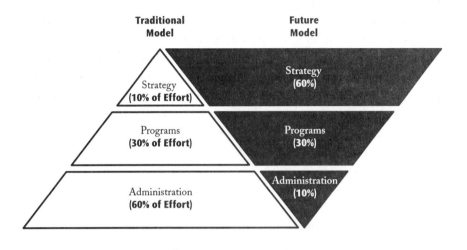

Traditional Model

Strategy (10% of Effort)

Programs (30% of Effort)

Administration (60% of Effort)

Future Model

Strategy (60%)

Programs (30%)

Administration (10%)

has had an administrative image and focused most of its resources and staff on routine, repetitive transactional activities. The role of HR as form processor, information provider, and general administrator is well known in most organizations. Although HR will remain responsible for many of these "personnel" activities, HR is asked to do much more today. Yet given the competitive climates that most organizations face, HR budgets are not increasing to keep pace with the increased demands. (For example, a recent Deloitte & Touche/Lawson survey found that 72% of HR respondents indicated that their HR staffing ratios are remaining the same or decreasing on an annual basis.) In essence, HR is being asked to do more with less. The model above captures the challenges facing HR in most organizations. (See Figure 13–1.)

In the past, HR functions focused on administrative responsibilities and the associated budgets, staffs, and resources. Because of that focus, less attention has been placed on developing value-added programs, activities, and resources; even less attention has been placed on the ways that HR and human capital can directly and indirectly affect firms' competitive positioning and strategy. Organizations no longer find that focus acceptable—to focus on administration risks such organizations' ability to outperform and outcompete the competition. It has been well documented that, in today's information-based, rapidly evolving global environment, people are seen as the competitive distinguisher between organizations in the way that production factors once were. As such, HR is being seen as the "owner," or entity, responsible for addressing human capital issues. To meet this expectation, HR must realign its priorities and focus on more strategic activities, including resource allocation. In many circles, this shift is described as the need of HR departments to become better strategic business partners to their organizations.

A strategic business partner is defined as having the ability to do the following:

- Effectively translate business requirements into HR issues
- Create high-performing cultures
- Create an environment in which human capital/development is linked to the profit and loss statement

In this vein, HR has looked toward shared services as a key factor in service delivery. By more efficiently and effectively organizing its resources, HR can better focus on value-added services and strategies. Shared services involve the creation of a new organization that balances corporatewide coordination with the needs of unique business requirements. Common support activities, processes, and services are performed through a shared service, whereas organizational mechanisms ensure that unique business requirements are identified, met, and supported. The consolidation of shared services allows for cost reductions and improved use of resources because fewer HR resources are required to perform activities that are no longer redundant. The consolidation and streamlining of administrative activities that result from shared services make more money available for more strategic HR activities.

Shared services is more than a cost-cutting exercise, however. Removing administrative responsibilities from those HR professionals focused on specific business units allows those individuals to perform a new kind of HR servicing. HR professionals are no longer positioned as dedicated administrators but strategists or consultants to the business units. Also, the term shared services is not synonymous with administrative consolidation. The unifying theme for shared services is commonality, not administration. As such, even high-value-added activities can be pooled through shared services if there is sufficient commonality to add benefit to the organization through "sharing." The benefits to be considered are not just cost savings: If creating shared services can increase customer focus, improve levels of expertise, or enhance organizational flexibility, the opportunities for shared services exist regardless of any cost implications.

In a Deloitte & Touche/Lawson Software survey, this finding was confirmed. Respondents indicated that HR-specific shared services were implemented more often to improve HR services (49%) than to reduce costs (27%).

## The Emerging Model for Human Resources

By definition, implementing HR shared services will require organizational change. That change will certainly affect the HR organization and may even reach beyond HR. Although there is no single blueprint for this realignment, finding an approach that best fits the organization is very important. The authors have seen the development of a general model that captures the emerging trend in HR shared services organizations and that is being used by a multitude of firms of various sizes and across industries.

### Three Primary Elements

The emerging HR shared services model has three primary elements: centers of excellence, business partners, and service delivery and administration. In a number of different organizations there has been a movement toward organizing HR functions, processes, and staff according to these three elements (although different labels may be used). Centers of excellence refers to those HR activities that are typically involved in designing and developing high-value-added HR programs, policies, and activities that are intended to be used throughout the organization. The centers of excellence are typically found where the most deeply specialized HR professionals reside although they are available to and called on by individuals throughout the organization. Business partners are also HR strategists, but instead of being organized centrally, they are aligned to specific business units. Business partners also focus on high-value-added activities, even though their focus is not on functional expertise. Instead, business partners are charged with providing consultative and strategic HR support directly to their respective business units. The roles and priorities of business partners can therefore vary by business unit. In contrast to individuals in the centers of excellence, business partners have deep understanding of their business units and broad understanding of HR concepts. Both centers of excellence and business partners play strategic HR roles—the former from an organizationwide perspective and the latter on a business unit basis.

The responsibility for the routine, administrative, and transactional aspects of HR is separate from the first two elements. This element of the HR function is called service delivery and administration. Because they are separated from administration, the first two elements are able to focus on strategy. The third element focuses on operational efficiency and customer service. A traditional problem with HR is that HR professionals must often play both strategist and administrator. The result is that the administration consumes so much time that it limits the amount and quality of the strategic support provided. Furthermore, because HR professionals are not focused solely on administration, they often fail to achieve the optimal level of process efficiency and customer service. By separating these activities from strategy, the first two elements can focus on their core responsibilities while service delivery and administration can focus on achieving operational excellence.

Figure 13–2 exhibits a three-tier model currently in use. This model was developed based on our firsthand experiences at a number of client organizations and on the general research and conversations we have had with HR professionals and executives in a variety of venues. Following that initial research, we have implemented a special study to validate the model. To do so, we contacted 12 companies from various industries that we had not previously examined. (The annual revenues for the organizations examined ranged from $3 billion to $27 billion, and total employees ranged from approximately 8,000 to 95,000. The HR organizations of these companies ranged from 50 to 1,400 individuals.) By speaking to HR leaders from each of these 12 organizations, we confirmed that the three-tier model is evolving within many corporations.

*Figure 13-2*

## Shared Services Operating Model

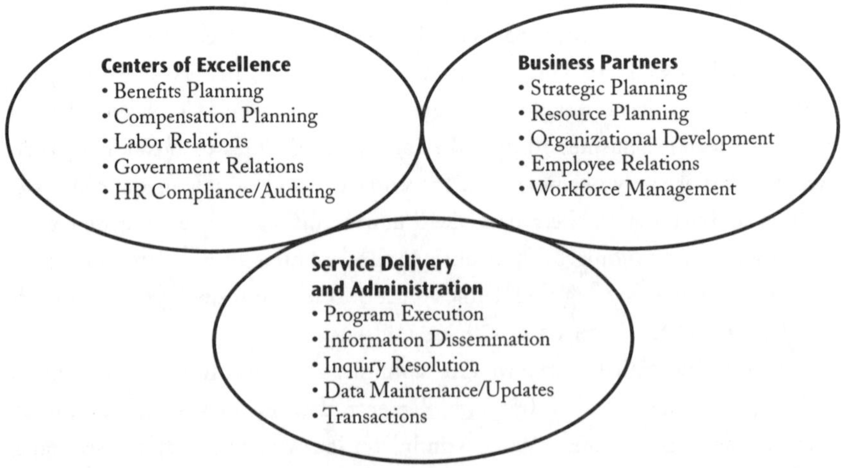

**Centers of Excellence**
• Benefits Planning
• Compensation Planning
• Labor Relations
• Government Relations
• HR Compliance/Auditing

**Business Partners**
• Strategic Planning
• Resource Planning
• Organizational Development
• Employee Relations
• Workforce Management

**Service Delivery and Administration**
• Program Execution
• Information Dissemination
• Inquiry Resolution
• Data Maintenance/Updates
• Transactions

Although companies may be at different stages, and the specifics of the model within each company can vary by title and role, our research validates this general framework. These companies in the study confirmed the desire to separate transactions and administration from strategic HR activities (often in support of the strategic business partner mission mentioned above). At the same time, companies are further separating strategic HR roles into those that must be aligned to meet specific, unique business requirements and those that must possess a more holistic, functional HR perspective.

We identified additional trends (subject to further qualification) in the way organizations are moving toward the emerging model:

- Several organizations that were described as having historically strong, central corporate structures are seeking ways to make their HR organizations more responsive to the needs of their business units. These companies are especially concerned with establishing organizational elements to foster a stronger business partner presence.
- Respondents in our sample that described their companies as historically decentralized or are recently experiencing significant merger and acquisition activity generally desire greater centralized centers of excellence, which would reduce costs and create a more uniform corporate identity.
- Nearly all the companies in our sample discussed the need for their organizations to streamline and centralize HR service delivery and administration and to separate such activities from more value-added HR activities. Toward this end, most of the companies in the sample are implementing service centers or other technologies aimed at more efficient provision of HR services.

Every organization that embraces HR shared services continually strives to find the organizational arrangement that works best. The model we have presented reflects the type of organization being developed in many HR functions and captures many of the trade-offs involved in designing an optimal HR organization (e.g., business focus versus corporatewide perspective, strategic role versus administrative role, and HR functional experts versus HR administrators).

## Critical Design Considerations

Regardless of the model sought by the organization, addressing a number of critical design considerations can help HR and corporate leaders determine which shared services model to deploy.

*Figure 13-3*

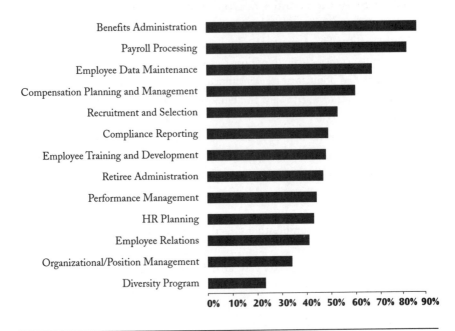

**Functions Provided or Expected to
Be Provided Through Shared Services**

The three-part model in Figure 13–2 depicts the organizational context or framework that is often used to deploy specific shared services operations. It usually comprises subsets of activities in either the centers of excellence or service delivery and administration, which are called the shared services operations, because they are performed throughout the organization.

### Determining Which Activities to Perform on a Shared Basis
Although shared services are often assumed to be administrative activities, almost any HR activity can be performed on a shared basis. The criteria for sharing is not whether the activity is administrative, but whether the activity can be shared in a manner that provides benefit to the organization as a whole and to specific business units. Historically, the most common functions that have been moved into shared operations are high-volume administrative activities such as benefits and payroll administration. Figure 13–3 shows which HR functions are most likely to be performed on a shared basis.

Generally, HR functions will begin migrating toward shared services by consolidating one or more of the most common services such as benefits, payroll, or data administration. Additional activities can be added throughout the evolution of the shared service. A number of criteria, including the following, can help evaluate and prioritize the services under consideration:

- Commonality. The first step in exploring shared services is to determine which HR activities are common across business units. These activities provide the initial population to consider for shared services.
- Volume. High-volume, repetitive functions are often the initial candidates for shared services.
- Uniqueness. The more unique the process or activity, and the more unique the requirements of each business unit, the less likely it is that an activity will be successfully performed on a shared basis.
- Complexity. Low complexity and highly regimented functions are normally considered for inclusion first, although complex, high-value services can also be provided on a shared basis if there is sufficient commonality across business operations.
- Cost impact. Consolidation of activities that yield higher cost savings (through economies of scale) are normally prime candidates for shared services.
- Compliance. Compliance and regulatory risks, in which inconsistencies across business units create exposure, can be reduced through shared services.
- Customer service. Activities with low current service and satisfaction levels provide a strong case for inclusion, especially when similar services are performed across multiple units.
- Feasibility. High transitional costs (hard and soft) and technology or data availability constraints can limit the effectiveness of shared services.
- Outsourcing. It may be more desirable to outsource a given activity rather than to consolidate it in a shared service.*
- Culture. Culture and other unique considerations may also affect the decision to consolidate.

---

*Note: Whether a specific activity should be outsourced is an entirely separate discussion than whether an activity should be performed on a shared basis. Because much has been written on outsourcing trends, alternatives, and pitfalls, this chapter will not revisit these issues. However, the HR professional should realize that shared services are neither synonymous with nor antithetical to outsourcing. Shared services can be achieved through, and can co-exist with, complete or partial outsourcing, although outsourcing alone does not necessarily provide the types of benefits to the organization that we have attributed to shared services.

A common misperception about shared services should be cleared up. Many people use the terms "shared services" and "service centers" synonymously. The misuse of terms often clouds a full appreciation of the range of activities that can be performed and the benefits that can be achieved through shared services. As described above, "shared services" refers to the creation of independent operating units charged with performing services that are common across multiple business units. The theory of shared services allows that both high-volume/transaction-based and high-value-added/experience-based support processes can be shared across an organization.

Service centers, also referred to as call centers, typically involve a centralized staff and the use of telephony, HR, and other technologies to provide primarily routine administrative and customer services to a customer audience. Service centers connote administration and transactions, but the theory of shared services is much broader. The best way to understand the two terms is to see shared services as the end and service centers as one means to achieving that end. In other words, service centers are merely one of the tools available in the design of shared services. Often shared activities, especially those equated with service delivery and administration, will be performed through a call center operation. However, there are numerous alternatives for providing such services, including automated, Internet-based self-services.

### Determining How to Deploy the Shared Services

An organization must determine what activities to perform on a shared basis as well as how to deploy those services into a shared services framework. When developing the model for a shared service implementation, the organization must decide

- What business units (or locations or divisions) will have services integrated into the shared service?
- What employee (or customer) groups will be serviced by the shared service?
- What staff will be realigned to the shared service?
- In what sequence will this migration occur?

The same criteria used to determine which activities to perform on a shared basis can be used to address how to deploy those activities. In so doing, companies may opt to add services, customers, and staff in stages or all at once in a "big bang." A big bang allows an organization to make a large change at once and to get a significant and immediate positive effect from its shared services implementation. Although some companies have been successful with the big bang approach, many other companies opt for a staged approach because of risks inherent in a big bang implementation. These risks include the following:

- Higher initial implementation costs and necessity for planning
- Visibility of initial problems to the entire organization
- Limited ability to make adjustments in shared services operations or strategy
- Perfection from the beginning is more critical because there is less ability to learn by doing
- Initial drop-off of service becomes more noticeable and more likely

An alternative staged approach allows the shared services organization to build its competency and size according to the following stages while the organization is gradually able to adapt to shared services:

- Pilot. An initial selection of shared services is implemented for a small segment of the organization. During this time, problems can be quickly identified and remedied before the organization continues to the next phase.
- Ramp-up. Piloted shared services are added and rolled out to progressively larger segments of the organization. Lessons learned during the pilot stage about shared services operations and communications are applied during the ramp-up stage.
- Continuous improvement. Once services are implemented, the shared services organization can expand and improve them. Service improvements can be reaped by addressing issues uncovered through assessment of shared services activities and through improved technology.

For example, one organization that we worked with began with a pilot phase that provided a set of key services to 20% of its population. During the ramp-up phase, the organization expanded the services to their entire company and then added more planned services to the shared services organization. The organization is currently focused on providing services to new acquisitions, streamlining HR processes, and adding technology that will increase service levels and customer satisfaction.

## Choosing a Governance Model

A critical question in shared services is always how the new organization will report within the organization. Because shared services must balance corporatewide and business unit–specific interests to be successful, the issue of governance is critical. It is common that centers of excellence will report through a corporate structure whereas business partners will report through their respective units. It is vital that sufficient cross-reporting and performance management occur to ensure that one element's priorities are not realized at the other's expense.

Often the most problematical element to address from a governance perspective is service delivery and administration. Unfortunately, the most common governance model has service delivery and administration report to the centers of excellence and thus into the corporate HR function. The common result of such a model is that the distinction between the centers of excellence and the service delivery and administration is often blurred. Centers of excellence often fail to maintain their focus on strategy and become involved in administrative issues whereas the service delivery and administration can become captive to more corporatewide concerns at the expense of a sufficient business focus.

A preferred governance model is to create a corporatewide (not function-specific) shared services umbrella group that is used to house all shared services operations, even functions beyond HR such as finance or information services. The advantage of the umbrella structure is that transactional and customer service skills, experience, processes, and technologies can be leveraged across all of these functions. At the same time, these shared services can focus purely on operational excellence without becoming overly captive to functional or business unit concerns.

When one is designing a governance model for shared operations, it is useful to consider which models will do the following:

- Be most consistent with overall corporate strategy and culture
- Most likely achieve expected and required benefits
- Provide the greatest efficiency and cost savings
- Provide the best customer service
- Minimize the degree of resistance experienced from executive leadership, staff, and employees in general
- Allow the function to best achieve its strategic objectives
- Best ensure legal and regulatory compliance in HR
- Best allow for future growth and expansion
- Enable integration with other support functions
- Meet the needs of the various business units

Another aspect to determining the scope and implementation plan for HR shared services is to determine whether business units will have discretion in using the services provided. As a means of encouraging shared services organizations to be externally competitive, business units may be allowed to opt out of services. In that case, the business unit is free to find an alternate provider that can provide equivalent services in a cheaper, more effective manner. However, because of economies of scale and the sensitivity and complexity of HR data, most companies mandate participation in shared services.

### Deciding Who Pays

Because the creation of a shared services operation often involves a significant investment at the start and the extraction of support activities from business units, a central question must be answered: How will the new service be paid for? Shared services often involve the promise of future cost reductions, so it is essential that cost mechanisms allow cost savings to be realized throughout the organization. Although technologies have allowed services to be charged in a number of different ways, the primary methods include the following:

- For profit. The shared service will charge business units for services according to external market rates and will attempt to operate "profitably." Market-based units of measures are used, and therefore the shared service must compete on the basis of price and service.
- For service allocation. The shared service allocates total operating costs to business units according to the proportion of actual services used by that entity.
- Break-even allocation. The service allocates all costs to business units according to divisional size, headcount, or some other general allocation method.
- Cost center. General overhead expenses charged to business units are adjusted to cover the costs of the service.

## Planning for Shared Services: Lessons and Approaches
### Pre-Implementation: Understanding the Business Imperative

Successful planning and implementation of shared services can be a formidable task. Whatever the specific corporate situation, understanding the business issues involved in a shared service initiative is a necessary first step before proceeding with implementation. Without a strong business justification, or "business case," it may be difficult to motivate the organization to make the changes and investments necessary to reach the desired end state. Even when a formal business case is not required, it may be helpful to conduct such an analysis to help focus up-front plans and goals and to avoid complications later in the implementation process.

Business cases can take many forms, but all successful reviews include accurate documentation of current performance and expected improvements. Typically, business cases involve a quantitative analysis that examines the financial benefits expected to be realized as a result of the initiative. The quantitative analysis often considers the costs of implementation as well as expected ongoing operating expenses as compared to the current state. Because shared services are not always financially driven, qualitative considerations can and should also be addressed. In instances in which the primary drivers are nonfinancial measures, it is especially important to highlight the qualitative benefits that shared services will provide to the organization, its business units, and its customers.

A business case serves as the general road map for the implementation and also functions as a strong communications tool to increase support among key stakeholders. In most organizations, successful business cases include the following:

- A vision for future operations
- A well-defined scope of expected services
- A high-level view of the implementation plan
- The expected financial and qualitative benefits
- Required implementation costs and resources
- Current performance metrics and future performance targets
- A clear statement of the changes required to make the initiative successful
- The important financial and operational assumptions used in developing the business case

A strong and supported business case used as a tool for developing and obtaining a high level of commitment can go a long way toward making the design and implementation of a shared services project successful.

## Implementation: Five Key Threads

Research indicates that there are nearly as many ways to implement shared services as there have been successful implementations (Deloitte Consulting/IDC, 1999). However, regardless of the implementation approach used, shared services can be seen as possessing the following five key threads that must be addressed simultaneously:

- Strategy
- People

- Process
- Technology
- Infrastructure

A successful shared services implementation requires a clear strategic perspective. It must be clear to all stakeholders how the shared services initiative supports overall business objectives and what types of benefits the change is expected to achieve. There must also be consensus regarding the role and design for the shared services. All stakeholders and involved parties must understand what the shared service will do and how it will perform in the desired future state. The final strategic element is a clear plan for implementing the design. The best strategies must integrate all of the additional threads described below and address the potential risks and challenges that the initiative may face along the way.

Staffing is a critical component to a shared service. Because the shared service often is a new entity, "clean slate" decisions must be made about the type of staff that is envisioned to support the desired end state. A common but significant issue is whether existing staff members will be transferred to the shared service or whether new staff members will be recruited to perform shared functions. Additional staffing issues include ways to compensate and reward staff members, appropriate performance management systems, training requirements, and career pathing.

At the heart of any shared services initiative is a process design issue. In essence, a shared service is about taking (in most cases) existing processes and realigning how they are performed and who performs them. As described previously, a central question is to determine what processes can and should be performed on a shared basis. Additional process- or operational-related questions include how to design processes for the future environment, how to realign roles and responsibilities, how to adjust process interfaces in the new environment, what types of performance measures must be monitored over time to support the desired future state, and what processes can be eliminated.

Shared services are about more than simply creating call centers, implementing ERP systems, or leveraging self-service tools. However, without some of the latest technologies, many of the efficiencies and improvements to be gained by shared services would be significantly diminished. Technologies, which are dependent on the specific design, include telephony, call routing and tracking, case management, knowledgebase, work flow, Internet/Intranet, self-service, document imaging, fax-back, HRIS/HRMS, data warehousing, and forecasting tools.

# Implementation of Shared Services: Five Key Threads

### Strategy
- Gain executive and business unit sponsorship and commitment early.
- Do not underestimate the time, energy, and resources it will take to change HR culture and inertia.
- Build a solid business case, but understand that making change will require a "leap of faith." There are no easy answers.
- Communicate, communicate, communicate.

### People
- Assemble cross-functional project teams with individuals who possess the appropriate skills and experience.
- Staff for the future. Hire staff on the basis of what the job will be, not what it is today.
- Redesign evaluation, performance, and compensation structures. Today's systems won't work in tomorrow's world.
- Promote training. It is the key to call center success.

### Process
- Start small and build on your successes. Do not take on more than you can accomplish.
- Assess which HR functions can and cannot be performed in house.
- Reengineer broken processes. Do not redeploy inefficient processes.
- Focus not on performing transactions faster but on removing transactions altogether. Self-service is key.

### Technology
- Acquire technologies according to business needs. Do not get fooled by "fad technologies."
- Do not operate in a vacuum. Use technologies that are consistent with the overall corporate information technology direction.
- Realize that technologies provide the most "bang for the buck"—but also the largest risks in terms of budgets and time lines.

### Infrastructure
- Conduct a thorough site selection based on sound, socialized criteria.
- Plan required capacity carefully for staff, technologies, and facilities by using historical volumes and forecasting models.
- Understand lead times involved with preparing facility space.

A tangible and intangible infrastructure will be required to make the shared service work. For example, shared services are often placed into new locations. These locations must be selected in a manner that supports the overall vision for the initiative and ensures that the needs of the business are met. The location itself must be designed in a manner that supports the people, process, and technology requirements. Infrastructure can also refer to such intangibles as ensuring that new organizational and governance structures are fully defined, communicated, and supported.

The box on page 154 highlights a few best practices or keys to success that occur across the five threads.

## Navigating Change

Beyond the five principal threads of any shared services implementation, one additional factor is worthy of note: how to manage and navigate change through the implementation process. The journey toward successful shared services is a long one, filled with many difficult decisions and choices. The magnitude of change involved in such efforts is often underestimated. Nearly 65% of the respondents in one study made the mistake of underestimating the complexity of managing change (Deloitte Consulting/IDC, 1999). Failing to manage such change can be catastrophic.

In addressing organizational change, the presence of strong executive management and sponsorship is critical. Without senior executives willing to make tough and potentially unpopular decisions, the shared service initiative would be in peril. However, no single process or approach will alleviate all the symptoms of dealing with change in the organization. Experience and research, though, have demonstrated a few basic guidelines that can make the journey more manageable, including the following ideas that are especially significant for a shared services environment:

- Build a customer focus from the ground up.
- Manage expectations of internal and external customers.
- Assess organizational risk factors at the beginning, and develop plans to mitigate them.
- Gain support from executives and other stakeholders early in the project and continue to communicate with them regularly.
- Create a business case that clearly outlines why the project will benefit the organization.
- Invest in training and monitor its effectiveness.

- Communicate early and often.
- Monitor and communicate performance.
- Maintain flexibility.
- Take advantage of "low-hanging fruit" and "quick wins" to build the momentum for success.

One common pitfall that often manifests itself during change management is to lose sight of why the organization even exists. Communication is critical to building a solid foundation for the new enterprise and to helping ensure that everyone understands and supports the larger mission, values, and goals of the new organization. A perspective often overlooked during the fervor of implementation is that of the internal customer. These stakeholders should be represented in the leadership ranks, and they should be consulted during the journey. Their input may keep the shared service enterprise on the right path. It is often the end users who can provide the most useful insights as to what will and will not work in the future environment. Furthermore, the opinions of the end users are typically given great weight in assessing the success or failure of a shared services implementation.

## References and Suggested Readings

American Productivity and Quality Center. (1997). *Reshaping the corporation: Emerging best practices in shared services.* Houston, TX.

Deloitte & Touche. (1999). *HR organizational allocation study.*

Deloitte & Touche, & Lawson Software. (1998). *HR trends and technologies survey.*

Deloitte Consulting, & International Data Corporation. (1999). *Shared services: Learning from success.* Framingham, MA.

Deloitte Consulting, & International Data Corporation. (1999). *Shared services: Maximizing returns on investment.* Framingham, MA.

Khan, S. (1997, January/February). Managing in turbulent times: The key to being a leading company. *Journal for Quality and Participation.*

Khan, S. (1994). *The people process.* Washington, DC: NAW.

Khan, S., & Parent, D. A. (1998, December). *Technology and the changing face of human resources.* Paper presented to IQPC, Orlando, FL.

Ulrich, D. (1997). *Human resource champions: The next agenda for adding value and delivering results.* Boston: Harvard Business School Press.

Ulrich, D., Losey, M. R., & Luke, G. (Eds.). (1997). *Tomorrow's HR management.* New York: John Wiley & Sons.

Ulrich, D. (1998). *Delivering results: A new mandate for human resource professionals.* Boston: Harvard Business School Press.

# Glossary

**360-Degree Feedback:** A process through which individuals receive feedback from others—typically their supervisor, peers, subordinates, and sometimes customers—whose good working relationships are key to the individual's effectiveness. It is called 360-degree feedback because an individual gets feedback from others above, below, and at the same level in the organization's hierarchy. Sometimes called multirater or multisource feedback.

**360-Degree Performance Appraisal:** Performance feedback obtained from supervisors, subordinates, peers, and internal and external customers.

**Adverse Impact:** A situation in which members of a particular race, sex, or ethnic group have a substantially lower rate of selection in hiring, promotion, or other employment decisions. This rate is 80% (4/5ths rule) of the nonprotected group.

**Analytical Survey:** Use of the data collected in a polling survey for statistical analysis.

**Aptitude Test:** The measurement of a person's general ability to learn or acquire a skill.

**Archival Data:** Research data that exist in the form of past organizational reports and historical records.

**Assessment Center:** A place where job candidates can be observed in simulated work situations.

**Autonomous Work Groups:** Work teams that have the authority to manage their own tasks and interpersonal processes as they carry out their work. Also called self-managing teams.

**Avoidable Separations:** Represents the portion of employee turnover that management has the most opportunity to control.

**Behavioral Modeling:** Viewing videotapes of appropriate and inappropriate behaviors, practicing the behaviors with a trainer (i.e., role-playing), and receiving taped feedback on the effectiveness of the practiced behaviors.

**Behavioral Observation Scale (BOS):** A standard for measuring the frequency with which an employee displays critical behaviors as reflected in the employee's performance appraisal.

**Behaviorally Anchored Rating Scale (BARS):** A standard for numerically scoring an employee's performance on critical incidents to create a performance appraisal.

**Benchmark Jobs:** Jobs that anchor salary data to the relevant market for the purpose of comparing similar jobs in different parts of organizations.

**Benchmarking:** The process of identifying, learning, and adapting outstanding practices and processes from any organization, anywhere in the world, to help the organization improve its performance (as defined by APQC). Benchmarking gathers the tacit knowledge (i.e., the know-how, judgments, and enablers) that explicit knowledge often misses.

**Best Practice:** An action selected by a systematic process that has been shown to produce superior results and that has been judged as exemplary, good, or successfully demonstrated. Best practices are adapted to fit a particular organization. There is no single best practice because "best" is not best for everyone. Every organization is different in some way—different missions, cultures, environments, and technologies (APQC).

**Business Case:** The process of analyzing the benefits of an option in view of the costs. The business case provides qualitative and quantitative information for making an informed decision.

**Business Partners:** HR strategists who are deployed to individual business units to provide high value, business-specific HR consulting, and workforce planning services.

**Case Studies:** In-depth, multifaceted studies of a particular organization or sub-unit within an organization.

**Center of Excellence:** The component of an HR shared services design that is focused on developing and deploying such HR programs as benefits planning, compensation design, and labor relations strategy across the entire enterprise.

**Central Tendency:** The measurement of mean, median, or mode in a sample.

**Central Tendency Error:** An error that occurs when a rater tends to put all ratees toward the middle of the rating scale.

**Code of Ethics or Code of Conduct:** Rules prescribing acceptable conduct that may be considered a formal, written expression of internal or in-house law.

**Concurrent Validity:** A form of criterion-related validity in which predictor and performance information are collected at the same time.

**Construct:** A theoretical characteristic or concept (e.g., intelligence, introversion, job satisfaction) that is not directly observable but inferred from observable behaviors.

**Constructive Feedback:** The process by which individuals share data about past performance in a developmental manner to reinforce desirable behaviors or to change undesirable behaviors. Constructive feedback is an essential characteristic of effective teamwork.

**Construct-Related Validity:** The extent to which a test measures a specific theoretical construct, characteristic, or trait.

**Content Domain:** A body of knowledge, skills, abilities, and other characteristics defined so that given knowledge of behaviors may be classified as included or excluded.

**Content Validity:** The degree to which a measurement device measures the intended job performance.

**Content-Related Validity:** The extent to which a predictor (e.g., measurement) is representative of the content domain of knowledge, skills, abilities, and other characteristics considered necessary to perform a particular job.

**Continuous Process:** Ongoing improvement of business processes in terms of quality, improvement, or cycle time (APQC).

**Control Group:** A group of employees or subjects who are not exposed to any kind of treatment or specific change in working conditions in an experimental design.

**Corporate Ethical Modeling:** A procedure that provides guidance on (1) appropriate and inappropriate behavior, (2) translating managerial beliefs into ethical behaviors, and (3) clarifying the organizational instrumentalities between the ethical behaviors and the rewards or punishments.

**Cost-Benefit Analysis:** A technique used to compare total resources required with total benefits from each program, system, service, unit, or activity.

**Criterion:** A measure of job performance or behavior such as productivity rate, accident rate, absenteeism, or supervisory ratings. Also, a standard against which predictor measures are evaluated.

**Criterion-Related Validity:** The extent to which predictor measurements (e.g., tests, assessments) are related to criterion measurements (e.g., job performance). Concurrent criterion-related validity is when the assessment instrument and the criterion are measured at approximately the same time; predictive criterion-related validity is when predictor information is collected and used to forecast or predict the criterion.

**Critical Incident Evaluation Method:** A narrative describing the employee's behaviors that have had a very positive or very negative effect on the organization.

**Critical Success Factors:** The (1) quantitative measures for effectiveness, economy, and efficiency; (2) those few areas where satisfactory performance is essential for a business to succeed; (3) the characteristics, conditions, or variables that have a direct influence on a customer's satisfaction with a specific business process; (4) the set of things that must be done right if a vision is to be achieved (APQC).

**Critical-Incident Method:** A method of job analysis that describes the setting, behaviors, and positive or negative consequences that resulted from a particular behavior as determined by subject matter experts.

**Cutoff Score:** A specified predictor score below which job candidates are rejected.

**Employee Stock Ownership Plan:** A philosophical belief in employee ownership. Such a plan may also provide an inexpensive way for employees to borrow money or be an additional employee benefit.

**Exempt Position:** A job for which the wage and hour provisions (e.g., overtime pay) of the Fair Labor Standards Act do not apply.

**Experimental Group:** A group of employees or subjects that actually receives some kind of treatment or change in working conditions in an experimental design.

**External Equity:** The means by which employees can compare their pay rates with the rates of employees in similar positions in other organizations.

**Fairness:** A social, not psychometric, concept based on the job, population, and use of predictor scores.

**False Negative:** An erroneous prediction that a person will fail, resulting in that person's rejection; however, the person would have succeeded if selected.

**False Positive:** An erroneous prediction that a person will succeed, resulting in that person's selection; however, the person actually fails to meet performance expectations.

**Focus Groups:** An information collection technique derived from marketing research where in-depth and interactive discussions with employees or subjects about issues of interest are conducted in a small group environment.

**Forced Choice Method:** An approach to performance appraisal that requires the rater to choose from statements designed to distinguish between successful and unsuccessful performance.

**Formative Evaluation:** A procedure conducted during various stages of a work cycle that is used to improve the work being performed.

**Functional Job Analysis:** A procedure developed by the U.S. Department of Labor that provides standardization for rating and comparing different jobs. The analysis concentrates on the work performed and on worker traits.

**Gain Sharing:** A philosophy of cooperation in which an involvement system is tied to a financial bonus.

**Graphic Rating Scale:** A series of scores that depict the employee's performance on a number of traits.

**Graphonalysis:** Handwriting analysis used to identify personality characteristics.

**Halo Effect:** A rating error in which the rater's overall impression of the ratee is based on one dimension of that ratee and not on the total dimensions of performance.

**HR Call Center:** A technology-supported, transaction-based entity designed to answer employee inquiries and to perform administrative functions in a variety of HR-related topics ranging from benefits to payroll.

**HR Call Center Technology:** The critical tools that aid in effectively answering employee inquiries in a call center environment, including a knowledge base, case management, integrated voice response, automatic call distributor, and skill-based routing.

**Human Resource Information Systems (HRIS):** Computerized networks or programs that can be used for the electronic collection, storage, retrieval, and analysis of organizational and individual data.

**Impairment Testing:** A test to detect actual impairment of motor skills and hand-eye coordination.

**In-Basket Exercise:** A behavioral test designed to evaluate certain skills in a controlled environment (usually administered during assessment activities).

**Informed and Voluntary Consent:** A requirement that researchers apprise potential participants about a study before the participants become involved in it. Participants should be advised that they have the right to withdraw their consent at any time during the research process.

**Internal Equity:** How employees view their pay in relation to others within the organization.

**Involuntary Turnover:** Separation from the unit as a result of the employer's action (e.g., a termination, discharge).

**Involuntary Turnover Rate:**

$$\frac{\text{Number of involuntary permanent separation}}{\text{Average number of employees for period}} \times 100 = \text{Turnover rate}$$

**Job Analysis:** A systematic process used to identify the tasks performed on a job and the knowledge, skills, abilities, and other characteristics (KSAO) required to perform the job.

**Job Description:** A brief description of the duties, responsibilities, and working conditions of a job.

**KSAO:** Knowledge, skills, abilities, and other characteristics.

**KSAs:** The knowledge, skills, and abilities of job applicants and employees.

**Leniency or Strictness Error:** A performance rating error in which the appraiser tends to give a group of employees unusually high or unusually low ratings.

**Likert Scale:** Graded responses to questions or statements in terms of five categories: strongly agree (SA), agree (A), undecided (U), disagree (D), and strongly disagree (SD).

**Management by Objectives (MBO):** A performance evaluation that begins and ends with the manager and the subordinate working together to set goals and objectives for the employee.

**Net Present Value (NPV):** The measurement of expected change in total stockholder wealth.

**Networking:** A system in which a parent company selects and trains volunteers to leave the parent company in order to establish their own businesses based at home, in community offices, or in independent locations. Company offshoots are connected to the parent company via computer.

**Non-Exempt Position:** A job for which the wage and hour provisions (e.g., overtime pay) of the Fair Labor Standards Act apply.

**Organizational Culture:** The shared philosophies, values, beliefs, norms, and attitudes that knit an organization together.

**Performance Appraisal:** A formal, structured system for measuring, evaluating, and improving an employee's job-related behaviors and output.

**Performance Measures:** Quantifiable core indicators of the effectiveness of an organizational unit or individual.

**Position Analysis Questionnaire (PAQ):** A structured questionnaire, consisting of 194 items, that quantitatively samples worker-oriented job elements, including information input, mental processes, work output, relationships with other persons, job context, and other job characteristics.

**Power Test:** Measurement without time limits of a person's expertise in a subject area.

**Predictive Validity:** The degree to which a measurement device predicts how well an employee will perform in the future.

**Predictor:** A measure used to predict criterion performance (e.g., scores on a test or the judgment of an interviewer). There are six categories of performance used in job selection: (1) psychological tests or inventories (general intelligence, interests, personality, ability); (2) work samples; (3) interviews (structured, unstructured); (4) biographical information; (5) peer assessments; and (6) situational exercises (in-basket).

**Pre-Employment Test:** A device used to assess through paper-and-pencil responses or simulated exercises a candidate's ability to perform a certain job.

**Preventable Turnover:** The movement of employees out of the organization or unit that the organization could have avoided. Preventable turnover may include separations that are classified as involuntary terminations, such as when employees are automatically terminated for failing to report to work or for failing to call to report the reason for their absence. Those employees may in fact have voluntarily resigned without notice. Preventable turnover may also exclude separations that are in fact voluntary but which the organization would not wish to prevent, such as retirement.

**Primacy and Recency Errors:** The results of heavily weighted incidents or information that either occur early in the review period or are very recent experiences.

**Primary Research:** Research projects in which the researcher is directly responsible for collecting data for or controlling how and what information is collected.

**Profit Sharing:** A bonus to employees that is based on percentage of the company's profits beyond some minimum level.

**Protected Group:** People who are covered by civil rights and equal employment opportunity legislation for employment opportunities. Such groups include women, ethnic minorities, persons with disabilities, and persons of certain ages.

**Quality Circles:** Small groups of volunteers who meet regularly to identify, analyze, and solve quality problems and other work-related issues.

**Relevant Labor Market:** A geographic area or areas where an organization would expect to recruit all potential employees for a job.

**Reliability:** A measure of the consistency in evaluation scores from one evaluation to the next.

**Reliability Coefficient:** The correlation between two or more performance evaluation scores.

**Response Time:** The period between the date of the job requisition and the date that the first qualified candidate is referred for an interview.

**Restriction of Range:** The situation in which a portion of a group is not used or selected after administering a test. The situation results in a group that has less variability in scores and is likely to have a lower correlation between predictor and criterion scores.

**Return on Investment:** The increased value of an amount invested over a stated period of time, often stated as net income divided by total assets (return on assets) or as net income divided by owners' equity (return on equity).

**Right to Privacy and Confidentiality:** "The right of the individual to decide the extent to which attitudes, opinions, behaviors, and personal facts will be shared with others."—Stone, E. F. (1978). *Research methods in organizational behavior* (p. 147). Santa Monica, CA: Goodyear Publishing.

**Scanlon Plan:** See Gain Sharing.

**Secondary Research:** The use of data or information that was initially conducted or gathered by other researchers or organizations.

**Selection Process:** The identification and matching of job applicants' qualifications to position requirements in order to choose the most competent candidate.

**Selection Ratio:** The number of job openings divided by the number of job applicants.

**Service Delivery and Administration:** The process of performing routine, administrative, and transactional HR activities for the entire organization, including payroll processing, status changes, benefits administration, and employee inquiries.

**Service Levels:** The key levels of support that the shared service center is responsible for delivering to business units across the organization. The key accountabilities are put in writing and widely disseminated via internal communication mechanisms to ensure clear expectations and accountability for performance.

**Shared Services:** The process of evaluating divisionalized business units engaged in diverse operations (such as HR, finance and information technology) to identify common processes for purposes of consolidating and delivering service on a shared basis.

**Shared Services Allocations and Charge-Backs:** The plan by which the shared financial, human, technology, and infrastructure costs will be accounted for among business units.

**Shared Services Governance:** The plan by which strategy will be set for the shared service, by whom, and within what reporting relationship.

**Shared Services Umbrella:** An independent operating entity that controls a set of common work processes for all business units, consisting not only of HR processes but also of finance and other functions.

**Speeded Test:** A test that measures processing speed for an activity.

**Stakeholder:** Any individual or group that has an interest in or is affected by the products and services delivered by the team being evaluated.

**Standard Deviation:** A measure of the deviation of scores about the mean (e.g., performance evaluation scores).

**Subject Matter Experts (SMEs):** Job incumbents, supervisors, or others with sufficient knowledge of a job to perform a job analysis.

**Summative Evaluation:** An appraisal conducted at the end of a work cycle and used to provide constructive feedback to the incumbent to improve future performance.

**Synergistic Organization:** An organizational unit with a highly integrated team that produces results greater than the sum of the results that could be produced by individuals functioning alone.

**Task-Oriented Job Analysis:** A study that focuses on the tasks rather than the behaviors involved in performing a job.

**Time to Fill:** The period between the date of the job requisition and the date on which the job offer is accepted by a qualified candidate.

**Time to Start:** The period between the date of the job requisition and the date on which the new employee starts to work.

**Turnover Analysis:** The use of turnover rates, proportions, and characteristics to determine relationships between organizational factors and the separation of employees.

**Turnover Rate:** The percentage of employee separations for a given time period that is the result of the following calculation:

$$\frac{\text{Number of permanent separations}}{\text{Average number of employees for period}} \times 100 = \text{Turnover rate}$$

Also called separation rate.

**Turnover:** Permanent movement of employees out of the organization or out of a unit of the organization, such as a department or a division. Turnover can be the result of resignation, termination, transfer, retirement, and so forth.

**Unavoidable Separations:** The portion of employee turnover over which the organization normally has no control.

**Validity:** The degree to which actions or inferences from scores are supported by evidence.

**Validity Coefficient:** The correlation between the performance evaluation score and some external measure, such as future work or training scores.

**Validity Generalization:** Evidence that the results of validity studies from one study may be applied to other situations involving one or more similar jobs.

**Value Added:** The increment to profit in a product that results from a trans-formational activity.

**Voluntary Turnover Rate:** Expressed as a percentage, the voluntary turnover rate is calculated as follows:

$$\frac{\text{Number of voluntary permanent separations}}{\text{Average number of employees for period}} \times 100 = \text{Turnover rate}$$

**Voluntary Turnover:** Separation from the unit that results from of the employee's decision (e.g., resignation, retirement).

**Work Sample Test:** A test that requires the applicant to perform tasks that are part of the actual work required on the job.

**Worker-Oriented Job Analysis:** A study that focuses on the behaviors involved in performing the job rather than on the tasks involved in the job. Sometimes called behavior-oriented job analysis.